THE MIND OF JOE

JOE DESHON

THESE ARE SOME RANDOM INSIGHTS INTO MY MIND.
IF YOU READ THIS, YOU'LL BE AMUSED, ENTERTAINED,
AND OCCASIONALLY ENRAGED.
BUT AT LEAST YOU'LL UNDERSTAND WHERE I'M COMING FROM.

Song lyrics contained within remain the property of their respective copyright owners. Fair use for reasons of commentary is claimed.

ISBN: 978-1727354515

Dedicated to the memory of my mother.

After all, if it weren't for her,
I wouldn't be here!

The Prelude

I always wanted to write. If I could actually earn a living doing this, it's what I would do for the rest of my life.

But, darn it, there just isn't that much market for what I do. And there are plenty of people that do it better than I do.

So I went for years with an unfulfilled need — the need to be heard.

Then a friend of mine introduced me to the wonderful world of "blogging". He told me that every night he spends 15 minutes before going to bed writing his innermost thoughts and posting them on the World Wide Web. Random thoughts. Things that happened during the day. Something that he read in the paper. Whatever.

What an intriguing concept! You get to write; you have a potential audience of billions; there's no accountability for what you write — no editor looking over your shoulder. Just you and your soul and a computer keyboard.

Thus, in the spring of 2006, "The Mind of Joe" was born.

It began with Judy Garland — my fond memories of my Dad's attraction to his silver-screen sweetheart. It continued with my fascination of Meg Ryan. And Julia Roberts. And (sigh) Karen Carpenter.

I wrote about my conservative political views. I did a fair share of liberal-bashing. I killed ants. I admired radio towers. I extolled capitalism.

I discovered that I couldn't just "write". I couldn't "scribble". I had to "compose". Each article had to be a tome, an epic, a masterpiece. It had to be through-composed; a beginning, a middle, an end. A message. A punch line.

Well, that got a little exhausting. And strangely exhilarating at the same time. I felt like I was making a difference in the world. And all this pent-up "stuff" inside me finally had a place to express itself.

After a few months of writing, I settled down to a more reasonable pace. Instead of demanding that I write a new article every evening, I just write when my fancy overtakes me. The backlog has been relieved. I can relax now.

I have collected some of my favorite essays in this book in honor of my mother's 80th birthday. Re-edited, in paper form, for your reading pleasure. I present my mind. It's always been an open book. Now, it is *literally*. I hope you enjoy it.

Joe DeShon
August 31, 2007

My Dad Loved Judy Garland

My dad was a huge fan of Judy Garland. When I was growing up, we had all her records. I honestly think he would have left Mom and married Judy Garland if he had a chance. Well, maybe not. But he really, really liked her.

In the movie "Broadway Melody" in 1937, she played a teenager who was madly in love with the movie star Clark Gable. In a classic scene from the movie, she writes a fan letter — a love letter, actually — to Mr. Gable (as she calls him). His picture is sitting on the desk and she gazes at it fondly as she sings of her love for him.

I heard the song on the radio today, and I thought I'd share the lyrics:

==============================

You Made Me Love You
words by Joseph McCarthy,
music by Jimmy Monaco
Arranged by Roger Edens, with special lyrics

Dear Mr. Gable,
I am writing this to you
and I hope that you will read it so you'll know
My heart beats like a hammer
and I stutter and I stammer
every time I see you at the picture show.
I guess I'm just another fan of yours
and I thought I'd write and tell you so.

You made me love you
I didn't wanna do it,
I didn't wanna do it.
You made me love you
And all the time you knew it,
I guess you always knew it.
You made me happy,
Sometimes you made me glad.
But there were times, sir,
You made me feel so sad.

You made me sigh 'cause
I didn't wanna tell you,
I didn't wanna tell you
I think you're grand, that's true
Yes I do, 'deed I do, you know I do.
I must tell you what I'm feeling
The very mention of your name
Sends my heart reeling.
You know you made me love you!

(dialogue)

Aw, gee, Mr. Gable, I don't wanna bother you!

I guess you got a lotta girls that tell you the same thing. And if you don't wanna read this, well, you don't have to.

But I just had to tell you about the time I saw you in "It Happened One Night". That was the first time I ever saw you, and I knew right then you were the nicest fella in the movies!

I guess it was 'cause you acted so, well, so natural like — not like a real actor at all, but just like any fella you'd meet at school or at a party.

Then one time I saw you in a picture with Joan Crawford, and I had to cry a little 'cause you loved her so much and you couldn't have her — not 'till the end of the picture, anyway.

And then one time I saw you in person. You were making a personal appearance at the theater, and I was standing there when you got out of your car, and you almost knocked me down!

Oh — but it wasn't your fault! Naw, I was in the way. But you looked at me, and you smiled. Yeah! You smiled right at me as if you meant it, and I cried all the way home just 'cause you smiled at me for being in your way!

Aw, I'll never forget it, Mr. Gable. Honest injun. You're my favorite actor!

(singing)

I don't care what happens,
Let the whole world stop.
As far as I'm concerned,
You'll always be the top,

’cause you know
You made me love you.

==============================

That song will always have special meaning for me. For one thing, it explains exactly what every person who understands “passion” in movies already knows: movies can make you laugh and they can make you cry and it’s all because you feel a connection with the character in the show.

Another reason it has special meaning for me is because everybody at some point in their lives have felt about someone exactly the same way Judy Garland’s character felt about Clark Gable. It’s very easy to identify with that.

Even as she was proclaiming her love for him, she was still very respectful of his stature. She calls him “Mr. Gable”. She calls him “sir”! It’s kinda like Mary Richards, who could never get past referring to Lou as “Mr. Grant”. It’s a delicate concession to the fact that the admiration — however intense — will never really be consummated.

I can imagine that, as my dad watched that movie, he was actually singing the same words in his mind to Judy Garland. She made him love her, even though he didn’t want to do it.

The Rolling Stones' Half Time Concert

I'm not a big football fan or a big Rolling Stones fan. But something that happened during the Rolling Stones' performance at the recent Super Bowl halftime show caught my attention. The Stones sang only three songs — all standards. It was a carefully orchestrated event, guaranteed not to offend anybody and to avoid any possibility of wardrobe malfunctions.

Before singing the last song, Mick Jagger said something like this: "Here's a song that we could have sung for Super Bowl One. But, hey, good things come to those who wait." And then he sang "I Can't Get No Satisfaction". That comment helped me put the Stones in historical perspective.

Yep, "Satisfaction" was written and recorded three years before the first Super Bowl. In fact, I think it's interesting that we are coming up on several 50-year anniversaries in the history of rock-and-roll. (Elvis Presley would be over 70 years old if he were still alive.)

Arguable the greatest rock band in history was The Beatles, but their height of popularity lasted only about five years, from 1964 to 1969. The Rolling Stones have been around for that long and have continuously remained popular and creative. Not many entertainers can claim that — certainly not in rock-and-roll.

I remember a few years ago when George Harrison died, a friend of mine commented, "Oh my God! Keith Richards has out-lived George Harrison!"

So ya gotta hand it to them. No matter what you think of them, the Rolling Stones certainly get credit for success and longevity. Very few people in any industry discover exactly what they want to do and then succeed at it year after year after year any better than Mick, Keith, and Charlie.

The Divinely-Inspired Word Count

My adventures into blogging have given me a new perspective on the world of free-lance writing. Since it's *my* blog, I'm going to share that perspective with you and you may or may not read it. That's what this is all about, right?

When I was in college, one of my teachers told us about a writing assignment he had accepted. He had written a unit of Sunday School literature for his church's denomination. What an honor! To interpret the Bible for the faithful. To write literature that would be studied simultaneously by the masses on a Sunday morning. To literally be the voice of the denomination for a brief moment in time.

Oh, and the assignment specified that he had to do it in exactly 675 words. Well, he could squeeze in 690 if he was really feeling verbose.

You see, the article had to come out even at the bottom of the page. That wasn't an option. Too much white space at the bottom of the page and the parishioners might feel cheated. If the article was too long, it would spill onto the next page and, well, we just can't have that, can we? A smaller or larger font was out of the question because, after all, we have our standards.

The practice is sarcastically known as the "divinely-inspired line count".

Editors! Can't live with 'em. Can't shoot 'em.

How many authors have lamented editors that have arbitrarily split or combined paragraphs to make things come out even at the end? Or who have mangled sentence structure to delete or insert words to eliminate widows and orphans?

How many authors have determined that they will never succumb to the banal wishes of editors, only to do so in order to be paid?

Ah, the life of a blogger. No editors. No line counts. Nobody telling me my article is too long or too short.

Oh, yeah, and no pay.

Oh, well, at least I can end the article any time I want to.

Hawaiians Learn Economics

State legislators in Hawaii got a lesson in capitalism recently. And it's a lesson that should be shared with the rest of the world. The lesson: *supply-and-demand works*.

Here's what happened:

Last year, the citizens of Hawaii were in a state of revolt. Gasoline prices were at an all time high. For a state that already pays the highest prices for just about everything, that was just too much to bear. How could they scoot around on those interstate highways in Hawaii if they couldn't afford to fill their tanks? Something must be done. The perpetually Democratic Hawaiian legislators were more than eager to act.

So they did what any good blue-state lawmakers would do. They increased government intervention into private market forces. Yep, the way to keep gas prices low was simply to pass laws that put ceilings on the price of gasoline.

But the lawmakers forgot that free-market enterprise is rarely a respecter of idiot laws.

Guess what happened? The price of gasoline went down — yes, down — *in the 48 states*. The sudden increase of prices had been simply the marketplace reacting to what it perceived to be a supply-and-demand force. Capitalists all over the world knew it would eventually self-correct. And it did.

Except in Hawaii.

What did the gasoline dealers in Hawaii do? They left their prices, uhm, high. Yeah, *high*. They were scared to death that they wouldn't be able to raise their prices at a later date. So they refused to lower them. Soon, the state that already was paying the highest prices for gasoline was paying prices that were 50% above the market level.

The legislators were confused. Waitaminnit. How can laws that are supposed to keep prices *low* actually *increase* prices?

Last week, after it was determined that their ridiculous policies had actually cost Hawaiian citizens $35 million dollars in excess gasoline costs, the red-faced, blue-state lawmakers hastily and overwhelmingly reversed their previous decision and repealed the law. The marketplace promptly and politely responded with lower gasoline prices.

Here's a lesson in Economics 101 for all liberal law makers. The definition of a commodity is a product that is so ubiquitous and so homogenous throughout the marketplace that it can only be differentiated by, well, price.

Gasoline is a commodity.

You don't mess with Mother Nature, Superman's cape, or a free-market economy.

California's Insane Law

California has long been known as the land of fruits and nuts. But nothing is fruitier or nuttier than the idiocy known as Proposition 65. It's a product of California's well-intended but out-of-control initiative proposal system, which takes the job of lawmaking out of the hands of lawmakers. It's not quite like putting the inmates in charge of the asylum, but this is as close as it gets.

Proposition 65 demands that companies that subject the population to cancer-causing agents inform the public that, uhm, they're being subjected to cancer-causing agent. Good enough. I recently completed a trip to California and saw it in action. It left no doubt in my mind why California continues to have some of the highest cost of living in the country.

I yanked myself from my Midwestern roots and traveled to San Francisco on business for a few days. I stayed at a prominent luxury hotel downtown. When I first entered the lobby, I was greeted with a sign that said that — pursuant to city ordinance — the lobby was a non-smoking area. Okay, cool. A lot of cities have restricted smoking in public areas. No problem.

When I checked in, the woman at the registration desk told me they had a non-smoking room available. Would that be okay? *Okay?* Heck, that's what I asked for. That way I wouldn't have to smell anybody else's smoke. (By the way, to all you smokers. You stink. Do you get that? *You stink.* Don't worry about heart disease or cancer or anything. Just remember: you stink.)

I went to the elevator and saw my first Proposition 65 notice:

> Warning: This area contains chemicals including tobacco smoke known to the state of California to cause cancer and birth defects or other reproductive harm.

That's right, folks. You heard it hear first. Walking in the lobby or sleeping in the rooms of this hotel won't hurt you. But if you breathe the air in the elevator lobby, *you could die!* And it must be true, because the State of California says so.

The absurdity of this law cannot be any more obvious. This was not a cheap sign; it's a classy hotel. A piece of my hotel bill helped pay for that sign. But even more ridiculous is all the logistics that go behind those signs.

The state is required to maintain an official web site to support the law. From the site, you can download an eight-page PDF document that helps you figure out how to conform to the law. The document first says that there is no "official" wording that the signs have to include. Then it goes on to tell you what the sign should include, how big the letters should be, where the sign should be, and on and on and on.

In spite of this, several national hotel chains have recently been fined as much as $50,000 each for not having appropriate signs. Who could have thought that hotels are so dangerous?

Pacific Gas & Electric recently included a notice in their customers' bills that they occasionally use sandblasting to clean their equipment and naturally-occurring silicon is on the list. Yup, you heard it here first. *Glass causes cancer.*

Left Coast Liberals have always confused good intentions with results. They have never realized the incredible impact of such insane legislation. The state has to maintain regulations. Companies have to keep up with those regulations. They have to post signs. They have to notify customers.

Who wins? Lawyers, bureaucrats, printers, and sign makes. Who loses? Taxpayers and consumers. (Hey, that's you and me.)

And guess what? Not one baby's life has ever been saved by legislation like this.

The Sum of All Human Knowledge

Anybody who has known me for more than 15 minutes knows that I'm a big fan of Wikipedia, the world's largest free online encyclopedia. I'm one of their editors and a frequent contributor to their effort. They have a rather lofty goal: to organize and make available to the world for free the sum amount of all human knowledge. So far they're doing a pretty good job of it. But I have a feeling that they still have some catching up to do.

The sum of all human knowledge is, well, it's a lot. We're getting smarter every day. And knowledge, by its very nature, is cumulative. That means I need to know everything that I have learned, plus everything that my parents learned, and so on back to the days of Adam and Eve. Or at least back until the time that mankind figured out that fried chicken tastes better than the feathery kind.

Let's think about a few ways to measure the sum of all human knowledge.

Twenty years ago, I was the manager of the computer system for a manufacturing company. I remember the day when we finally bought enough disk space for our mainframe computer (Boy, there's a term you don't hear much any more – ask your teenager what a "mainframe" is.) so that now we actually had a full gigabyte of storage. That's it. A gig. One.

But we couldn't fit this gigabyte of silicon in one physical drive. No, we had to chain together three separate units, each the size of a washing machine, to reach that milestone. Three washing machines; one gig.

Under the desk where I'm sitting now there is 1,000 times that storage capacity in a space smaller than a shoebox. And it cost less than one-fourth as much as that 1985 gigabyte did – in pre-inflation adjusted dollars.

Such advancements in technology are almost impossible to imagine. Let's put it another way.

A Mersenne prime number is a prime number that can be represented by one less than two raised to the power of a prime number. (Did you get that? I think the sum of all human knowledge is increased every time I explain that definition to somebody.) It's one of those "Holy Grails" of computing. For years scientists have sought to spin electrons as fast as possible in search of larger and larger Mersenne Primes.

In 1952, the largest Mersenne Prime known to exist contained 157 digits. That's a pretty big number — larger than I want to count in my lifetime. But it got bigger and bigger every year.

By 1957, they had found one that was 969 digits long. By 1963, they finally found one that was 3376 digits.

Last year, scientists found a Mersenne prime that was 9,152,052 digits long. Almost ten million digits! If you wanted to "say" that number, you'd have to speak for eight hours a day for 28 days.

Here's the way I like to look at it. If the sum of all human knowledge twenty years ago was the size of a baseball and could be held in your hand, the sum of all human knowledge today would be about the size of a four-story office building. And it would cost about as much as a cup of coffee to store that knowledge on a smart stick that you could fit on your key ring. (You get the idea.)

Not only are we learning more, we are learning more at a faster rate. I remember my high school algebra teach mentioning something about geometric progressions. Funny thing about those geometrics, they tend to become almost vertical after a while.

Aren't we just about ready to go into orbit?

Inside-Out Writing

Once I saw an interview of some of the head writers for the old "I Love Lucy" show. They talked about how they always wrote the show "backwards".

They would begin with a situation and figure out how to get Lucy and Ethel there. For example, they figured it would be funny to have the girls tromping barefoot through a vat of grapes. Or they thought it would be funny to have them wreaking havoc in a candy factory. Then they would write a plot that would put them in that mess.

That's good advice. It's pretty close to Stephen Covey's "Habit Number 2": "Begin with the end in mind."

When I took a creative writing class, the teacher once gave us an assignment to describe a room two different ways. First, we were to go from general to specific: it was a big room, bright, with large windows, and a rug in the middle of the room with a table covered with a green table cloth and on top of the table was a pitcher of water.

Then we were to describe the same room going from specific to general: start with the pitcher of water and work out to a large, bright room. You get the idea.

The lesson was that it was possible to describe from either the general to the specific or the specific to the general. But it was important that you did one or the other and that you knew which direction you were going.

That's also good advice.

I have discovered that the two hardest things to write are the beginning and the end. So I usually start out in the middle and work my way out. Again, it doesn't matter what I do, as long as I am consciously doing it and I'm consistent. I call it my "inside-out" writing style. (Sometimes I write "outside-in", but the concept is still the same.)

I begin with the general idea of what I'm wanting to say (in this case, describe my writing style). Then I write the beginning (an anecdote about how "I Love Lucy" was written). Finally, I figure out a witty way to close, usually with some punch line.

It's kinda like that old joke:

Roses are red,
Violets are blue.
Most poems rhyme,
But this one doesn't.

In other words, if you were looking for a witty punch line right here...

Well, I didn't write one this time.

You Can't Cool a Kitchen with a Refrigerator

Here's a teaser that's a favorite of engineering students.

On a hot summer day, can you cool your kitchen by leaving the refrigerator door open?

The answer is nope. If anything, that will actually make your kitchen *warmer*, not cooler.

But how can this be? I thought you'd never ask.

The fact is, there is really no such thing as "cold". It's merely the absence of "heat". Refrigerators don't actually make things cold, they just remove the heat from them. And all that heat energy has to go somewhere. So it's usually just dissipated back into the room. Ever wonder why the coils on the back of your refrigerator are so warm? That's because they're busy getting rid of all that heat.

If you leave the door open, the refrigerator will have to work harder because it will have to remove the heat from the entire room, not just the inside of the refrigerator. And it will put the heat right back into the room, making it warmer.

That's the principle on which heat pumps work. They're just air conditioners in reverse, removing the heat from the outside and depositing it in the house. In the summer they reverse the cycle and take the heat out of the house and put it on the rose bushes next to my front porch. (Oh, *that's* why those bushes always look, uhm, tuckered out.)

Here's something even better. A ceiling fan doesn't make a room cooler. It just moves the air around. Moving air over our sweaty body feels cooler than stagnant air on our stinking body.

Actually, our engineering friends will tell us, it's possible that a ceiling fan will make the room *warmer*, because the fan motor is generating heat, which it then distributes around the room. Oh, great, that made me feel better.

Engineers also like to talk about the fact that helium balloons don't actually *rise*. Rather, the heavier air "pushes" them up. That's a subtlety that escapes most of us romanticists. Next thing they'll be telling us is that the Man in the Moon isn't really winking at me.

Creationists Create Wry Arguments

When creationists and evolutionists argue with each other, metaphors, analogies, and similes fly faster than Dan Rather fleeing from accusations of forged documents.

The creationists are especially creative and witty. One of my favorites was when biologist Edwin Conklin said, "The probability of life originating from accident is comparable to the probability of the Unabridged Dictionary resulting from an explosion in a printing shop." I really doubt that Professor Conklin actually calculated the probability of such a work of literature resulting from such an explosion. I think he was just trying to make a point of absurdity.

Actually, I thought that the correct absurd comparison had something to do with a room full of monkeys typing the complete works of Shakespeare. Now *there's* a thought!

I've often thought about hooking up a random-number generator to a PHP program and making millions of dollars with a web site that claims to read tarot cards. Don't laugh; it's been done.

Back to the creationists. Cambridge University's Sir Fred Hoyle once said that the chance of a simple cell evolving from primordial soup was about the same as a tornado passing through a junkyard and producing a fully functional Boeing 747. Ya gotta admit, that'd be pretty hard to imagine. A two-seater Cessna, perhaps. But not a 747!

Here's another one. Hoyle also compared the chance of obtaining even a single functioning protein from the random combination of amino acids to a solar system full of blind men solving Rubik's Cube simultaneously. Yikes. I'm sure a solar system full of blind men could eventually type Shakespeare, so I suppose each of them could eventually solve Rubik. But, doing it all at the same time? Man, I'd like to see that.

Heck, I'd like to see *myself* solve it just once. My son got "Instant Insanity" for Christmas last year and I'm scared to even remove it from the plastic box it came in. ("No, just leave it in there, son. It's a work of art. If you ever remove it, you'll never see it in that pristine state again.")

Evolutionists don't like this in-your-face kind of humor. They claim they are "straw men" arguments, which refers to the practice of setting up a weak argument, defeating it, and then claiming victory over your enemy. It would be like two men who are in a fight where one builds a man from straw, throws punches at it, and says he beat up the other guy.

Gee, that would be like throwing a deck of cards up in the air and having them land on the ground all neatly forming a mosaic of the Mona Lisa.

Eh. Maybe this analogy stuff should be left to the professionals.

Why Paris Hilton is Rich and Famous

Paris Hilton is a phenomenon that defies explanation. I've heard of a "death" spiral. But she seems to be — in spite of her best intentions — spiraling *upwards*. Go figure.

Originally, she was famous just because she was rich. Now she seems to be getting richer just because she's famous. Knock-down good looks helps, of course. But apparent lack of talent doesn't seem to be hurting her cause. Can she do anything wrong?

I think her best "asset" (and I must tread carefully here) is her name. It's a marketer's dream. Think of it.

Paris: The most beautiful and romantic city in the world. France doesn't deserve such a gem, but I'll save that for a later posting.

Hilton: A surname that literally exudes high-class and luxury with a rich, unspoiled history.

Can you imagine the conversation her parents had?

"Honey, I'm pregnant."

"Oh, good, now we can finally use that girl's name that worked so well in the focus groups."

"We're going to name our baby 'Las Vegas'?"

"Yup. That way she can never embarrass us. Because, after all, what happens with Las Vegas, stays with Las Vegas."

Mr. and Mrs. Hilton later changed their minds, Paris made her video, and the world has never been the same.

Oh, the Money that Dead Celebrities Make!

What do the King of rock 'n roll and the creator of the world's most lovable loser have in common with two ex-Beatles?

Elvis Presley, Charles Shultz, John Lennon, and George Harrison all made the most recent list of the world's highest paid dead celebrities, as compiled annually by Forbes magazine.

Also making the list this year were Ray Charles, Johnny Cash, Bob Marley, Marlon Brando, Andy Warhol, and 43-year-dead Marilyn Monroe.

Forbes even went on a limb to calculate the potential earnings of William Shakespeare, if only he hadn't been so careless to allow his copyrights to slip. Bill the Bard would have earned $15 million dollars last year in royalties for the wherefores in his plays and poetry — a mere pittance to The King's $45 million for his hip-gyrating antics.

Of course none of these people actually did any work last year. They were too busy decomposing. The wealth was generated on behalf of the heirs to their estates — who work vigorously to guarantee that no dead man's work be un-honored, and no royalty be unpaid.

In my opinion, the guy who has lost the most is King James, of KJV fame. If today's copyright standards had been in place in the 17th Century, James would now be famous as the guy who held the copyright on the Lord's Prayer and on John 3:16. Imagine what his heirs could have done with the royalties from every mention of the famous salvation passage on national TV by a hippie with clown hair in the end zone of a playoff game. Instead, the monarch is noted as the one who made "hallowed" a three-syllable word.

Remembering the 70s through Music

Ah, Bread. What wonderful memories. "Diary" was a nice song. But it's a song about a lost love. I'd rather look at a song of unfailing, unconditional love.

Here's the second verse of a classic:

==============================

If
by David Gates

If a man could be two places at one time,
I'd be with you.
Tomorrow and today, beside you all the way.
If the world should stop revolving spinning slowly down to die,
I'd spend the end with you.
And when the world was through,
Then one by one the stars would all go out,
Then you and I would simply fly away.

==============================

Read that to yourself real slowly. You just gotta cry.

The 70s were like a huge sigh of relief that the 60s were finally over. The 60s were dreadful. It seemed like everything was falling apart. But by the 70s, we were kinda turning a corner and it seemed like maybe things were going to be okay.

The war was winding down. We were losing it, but we didn't care. We had landed a man on the

Moon — been there, done that. Americans were going into space somewhat regularly, and occasionally meeting up with Russians once they got there. Inflation was in double digits. And gas prices were (gasp) approaching a dollar a gallon. But, hey, we had a president that was telling us that he couldn't do anything about it, and we just kinda adjusted our salaries and kept going. It was a very naive time.

And the music reflected it. Songs of the 60s were dirty, were radical. But in the 70s, they turned sweet. In the 60s, they sang about love, but they really meant sex. In the 70s, they sang about love and they really meant commitment.

Suddenly, television was in color! I remember our first color TV. We got it somewhere around 1972. We lived in a little town and could only get three stations with lousy reception. I remember that I was amazed that even the "snow" on the TV was in color!

A few years ago, I bought a new car with a really nice CD player in it. One of the first things I did was buy a CD of The Carpenter's greatest hits. It was wonderful. Karen Carpenter could melt my heart just by smiling, let alone by singing love songs. When she sang "Just like me, they long to be close to you" she was singing to ***me!***

That Labor Day, everybody was at my mother's house. I told my brother we were going to go for a ride through town in my new car. Actually, I just wanted to get him alone with Karen Carpenter. Yep, I popped the CD in, his face beamed, and we sang every word of every song together.

Music from the 70s was sweet and mushy, just like chocolate pudding. And that's the way I want to remember it.

When a Lawyer Writes a Web Site

When a company places a statement of policy on their corporate web site, they really should take a close look at it to make sure their message matches their intent. I recently discovered a boast that ended up sounding like a disclaimer which was in fact a promise to deliver inferior service.

As a web developer, I often randomly scour the Internet for inspiration. I pick up ideas here and there and incorporate them into — I mean steal them for — my own creative efforts. I search for both form and content, looking for the best and the worst of both.

It was during one such random wandering that I stumbled on the web site of — well, maybe I had better keep the name of the company confidential. After all, it was a law office. The last thing this struggling webmaster needs is a bunch of attorneys mad at him!

Here's what the notice said:

> Because of our philosophy of service, attorneys and staff at our law firm are accessible by regular appointments which are available between 9:00 a.m. and 5:00 p.m., Monday through Friday.

Hmmm. Just what is "our philosophy of service"? Surely they intended to imply their philosophy of *superior* service. Or at least *good* service. Didn't they?

So I looked all over the site. Nope, no claim was made anywhere on the site that offered service better than their competitors. Heck, they barely offered *any* service at all.

Okay, so the lawyers aren't going to make any claims that they can't deliver on. I guess we should expect that. So let's take it at face value. They're going to offer, uhm, service. Just that. They have a philosophy, and that philosophy is to do what they're supposed to do.

Let's continue.

They're available at "regular appointments", eh? You'd better call ahead, because if you just walk in off the streets, these guys aren't going to see you — even if they're just hanging around the water cooler talking about the next ambulance they're going to chase. Nope, you gotta have an *appointment*. Oh, not just any appointment will do. It has to be a "regular" appointment.

But wait, *there's more!*

Just when can you expect to make that "regular" appointment? Why, on their schedule, of course. They work nine-to-five, five days a week. Period. They're sorry if that's inconveniently at the same time that you're supposed to be earning an honest living. They can't help it that the mortgage company down the street boasts of their evening and weekend extended hours. They're sorry that my insurance agent will drive across town to meet me in my office to get my signature on a policy. No, if you need their legal advice, you'd better ask your questions during their 8-hour window.

As an aside, a few years ago, I had some legal work done (not by *this* firm) and I was surprised when I got the bill that I was charged $35 by my lawyer to read an email that I had sent him. Gosh, if I'd known that, I would have included a chocolate chip cookie recipe in the email to give it at least some semblance of value. (Lawyers are the only ones that can send you a Christmas card and then charge you for the stamp.)

So, this law firm started with what should have been an opportunity to differentiate themselves from their competitors, turned it into legal mumbo-jumbo that defies reason, and ended up bragging about the fact that they offer their services under utterly crummy conditions.

Some people think I think about things too much.

Hockey is a Stupid Sport

Recently, a friend of mine encouraged me to become a hockey fan. "It's the fastest game in the world!" he exclaimed.

Hah!

Maybe he was referring to the speed of the puck, that flat, poor-excuse-for-a-ball — the size of a ham sandwich — that they use in the sport. Heck, when I watch hockey on television, the snow on the screen is larger than the puck. The fact that it moves so fast is hardly something to be proud of. After all, I don't go to skeet-shooting competitions to watch the bullet glide through the air. Why should I watch a hockey game when the puck slides across the ice at about the same speed as a 747 at takeoff?

Maybe he was talking about the speed at which a forearm hits another guy's face. I guess that would be exciting if it was legal. I mean, isn't the idea to get the ball — I mean, puck — in that little net thing at the end? If you put an elbow in somebody's ribs, you should have to go sulk in timeout or something, shouldn't you?

And that's another thing. You know why hockey games are so low-scoring? Because the net is too small. The idea is to move the ball — I mean, puck — down the field — I mean, the ice — and deposit it in a little net with a 300-pound gorilla standing in front of it. Isn't that called goal-tending? Wait a minute, that's basketball. But isn't that illegal? More timeout time, I guess.

Anyway they shouldn't make them put it in a net; just crossing the end-zone line should be enough. It works for football. You can cross the plane of the goal line anywhere between the two out-of-bounds lines and it counts. Even in baseball, you can hit it anywhere between the foul poles. But no, in hockey, they give you a target the size of a car door.

But I digress.

Maybe he was talking about the speed of the action. Yeah, that's it. A game that ends with a score of 1-0 is exciting because it has a lot of *action* in it. Uh-huh. Sounds like a soccer score, and that's not any better. At least with soccer, the ball is the size of a cabbage so you can see it. And those little kids look so cute in their shorts. Oh, do grown men play soccer, too? I didn't know that.

Sorry, hockey is not the fastest game in the world. Nor is it the most exciting. Nor is it one that makes any sense at all.

People can't even *play* hockey, they can only *watch* it. When you were growing up, did your neighborhood friends ever knock on your door in the middle of July and invite you to play in a pick-up hockey game on the school grounds? Heck, they didn't even do that in January.

Nope, hockey is a stupid, wimpy sport. Everything I need to know about sports I learned by watching Tom Landry coach the Cowboys from the sidelines. When his guys got into a fight on the field, did he throw trash cans on the field? No, he stood there with his arms crossed and a scowl on his face.

Now, *there's* a real man in a real sport.

Waitaminnit, Who Died?

We were getting ready to start a meeting at work and, as is our habit, we were making small talk around the table while we waited for others to join.

Somebody mentioned that actress Maureen Stapleton had died and the newspapers were filled with accolades for her. Yeah, I said, but I couldn't believe that the papers were leaving out some of her best stuff.

The papers mentioned her role in *Lonelyhearts*, for which she earned her first Academy Award nomination for Best Supporting Actress. And she was nominated her work in *Airport* and in *Interiors*. And she won an Oscar for *Reds* in 1981.

But what about her work as the adorable dingbat Edith Bunker in *All in the Family*? That was never mentioned. That was the highlight of her career. Come on, you can't forget that one!

And what about her recurring role in *Scarecrow and Mrs. King*? And her great work with Meg Ryan in *You've Got Mail*?

And for Heaven's sake, what about all the work she had done on Broadway? And...

Oh, it was *Maureen* Stapleton that died? *Jean* Stapleton is still very much alive. Ooops.

Do you remember that *Saturday Night Live* skit with Gilda Radner as Emily Litella? She was always concerned about the government keeping a list of all the endangered feces on the planet. And they were always worried about too much sax and violins on television. And the Supreme Court was going to rule on the deaf penalty.

Well, it was kinda like that.

What's the King Doing?

A friend of mine is a man of modest means. But he enjoys his vacations. His favorite witty remark while on these escapades is, "I wonder what the poor people are doing right now?"

Of course, that's intended to be ironic. In a feat of self-envy, he *is* one of the poor people that he's talking about. But for a week or two out of each year, he puts his hard-earned savings to work and lives like a king. He knows that the next Monday he'll be back at the grind. But he's going to enjoy the luxuries of resort living while he can.

King Arthur felt the exact same trappings in the Broadway musical *Camelot*, but in reverse! Anxious over his pending arranged marriage to Guenevere, he paces the forest and hypothetically ponders "I wonder what the king is doing tonight". In his soliloquy, he assumes the role of the peasant who enviously gazes at the palace. Then he answers his own question:

> He's scared!
> He's numb! He shakes!
> He quails! He quakes!
> *That's* what the King is doing tonight!

The king — with all his riches — is actually longing to be a commoner, who obviously has no problems at all. And my friend wishes to be rich, so he could wonder what it's like to have all the problems of the poor people.

It's a paradox that defies reason: The grass is always greener — no matter which side of the fence you are on.

QWERTY, VHS, and Backslashes

Many times, the thing that seems to make the most sense isn't the thing that is finally accepted as universal.

Consider the QWERTY keyboard for a moment. We've all heard the story. The common layout of most computer keyboards is a dinosaur, left over from manual typewriters. The purpose was to slow typists down so the key bars wouldn't get jammed together on their path toward striking the paper. But even the concept of "striking the paper" is foreign to many computer users today. Why does this relic continue when more efficient key mappings exist? It's a mystery.

Another example is the VHS system of video tapes. In the early 1980s, everybody knew that Sony's Betamax system offered superior picture quality. Why did the VHS system prevail in the marketplace? It's a mystery.

But the best — or worst — example is the lowly backslash. In a feat of planned obsolescence that only the computer software industry could get away with, Microsoft's DOS Version 1.0 supported only floppy disks with a flat file structure — no directory systems were allowed.

Can you smell an upgrade coming? Sure! When the PC XT showed up with its (gasp) 10 meg hard drive, we couldn't put all those files on one directory. But Bill Gates and his wise men had already allocated the forward slash to indicate DOS command line switches. (Now, if you don't know what a DOS command line switch is, never mind. It's something us old people used to be concerned with before computers had mouses.)

Unix and that *eeevil* rival operating system CP/M used the dash for their command line switches. Bill had to be different, so he chose the slash. Dash, slash, who cares? Well, we all cared when we needed something to indicate directories. The slash was already taken. And the period was being used to distinguish the file extension.

What's a systems programmer to do? Close your eyes, point to the keyboard and land on the backslash, that's what. (Maybe they'll never notice and we'll get away with it.)

That's why the World Wide Web — which mostly runs on Unix computers — uses forward slashes for URLs, while Windows — which is just a prettied-up version of DOS — uses backward slashes for their directory names.

Hmmm... That explains backslashes. Can anybody actually explain the purpose of the grave, tilde, broken vertical bar, and curly brackets?

Nope, they're still mysteries.

A Thought about Withholding

This is the time of year I take a real close look at my finances because I'm suddenly aware of pay raises, taxes, performance bonuses — stuff like that.

I know, you're supposed to look at that stuff all the time. But most of us "regular" people are stuck with that evil known as "withholding". That makes things like taxes too darned transparent for our own good.

Generally, I'm not in favor of increasing federal regulations, but I'd like to propose one that may have some merit.

Employers are required to provide an itemized pay stub showing all the deductions every pay period. What if we made a federal requirement that those pay stubs also had to include the *percentage* of each deduction, when divided into the gross pay?

I think people have become rather immune to the fact that they pay "hundreds of dollars" every week to the government. But they have no idea how much of their pay is actually being taken away. I saw a survey one time that said most people think the number is somewhere around 25% — and they think that's too high.

I just dumped my most recent pay stub into Excel and did some math. My tax deductions equal 34.7% of my pay. I contribute 10% to my 401k, which leaves me with just a little over half of my paycheck remaining.

Printing those percentages on everybody's paystub may be a good "primer" toward getting what we really need — a flat tax.

To Pluto and Beyond

I've always been interested in space stuff. I grew up with the Gemini and Apollo missions. I always wanted to be an astronaut, but I knew I probably wouldn't be able to be one. So I just decided to devote my life to learning everything I could about space.

I remember being kinda disappointed when we finally landed on the moon. We had studied the moon from afar for years — peering at it through telescopes and wondering what it was really like. But when we got there, the astronauts weren't astronauts any more — they were geologists. Sheesh, that's no fun. It's a whole lot more fun to study another planet vicariously through a telescope or by an orbiter or lander. But to actually scoop up rocks and look at them under a microscope — gee, you could do *that* on Earth!

I got really excited a few months ago when I first learned about the New Horizons spacecraft. It's going to be the first spacecraft to actually visit Pluto and study it up close. Pluto is the last planet (of the original nine) that we haven't explored at all. And now they are discovering a whole bunch of cold, icy, rocky masses beyond the orbit of Pluto — some of which are planets in their own right.

I watched the liftoff on streaming video on NASA-TV while I was sitting at my desk at work. The Internet is a wonderful thing! It was just like the Apollo days. I felt like I was 13 years old again. I kept it running in a corner of my screen while I was doing my other work.

High surface winds at the launch site scrubbed the mission just two and a half minutes before it was to take off. But they were able to launch it successfully the next day. It was the most exciting part of my day. Everything else is pretty boring when compared to exploring an alien word thirty billion miles away.

The craft is well on its way to Pluto now, calmly coasting toward a rendezvous with Jupiter next year for a gravity assist. Then it's almost another decade of coasting until it reaches its target.

But who's in a hurry? Pluto has been there for a few million years. And it's waited for half a century of space travel. It can wait a decade or so more before it shows its face closeup for the first time.

Kirby and Dana

Within 24 hours of each other, two notable Americans were cut down in what should have been the prime of their lives. How could I *not* write about them today?

Kirby Puckett literally defined Minnesota Twins baseball for much of the 1980s and 1990s. He had forearms that were larger than most people's thighs. When he hit the ball, the hide would fly into orbit along with the core. His legacy included Golden Gloves, All-Star Games, batting titles, and World Championships.

His career was cut short when he was forced to retire at age 34, suffering from glaucoma. His entry into the Baseball Hall of Fame was a cakewalk, achieved on the first ballot during his first year of eligibility.

His personal troubles later in life included failing health, weight gain, and a few run-ins with the law. But during his professional career, he was a baseball player's baseball player, a gentleman on the field and a model citizen off. Who didn't like Kirby Puckett?

He suffered a massive stroke over the weekend and died the next day at his home in Phoenix. He'll be missed.

Dana Reeve was the perfect wife that every man could dream of. Already a talented singer and actress when Christopher Reeve found her and married her, they led the model family life, living far from trappings of Hollywood in suburban New York.

When Christopher was paralyzed from a riding accident, it was Dana who gamely faced the cameras and the media. In demonstrating her un-dying support for her husband, she exhibited grace, poise, and optimism that others could only dream to duplicate.

Dana and Chris (as she called him) always believed with all their heart that he would walk again. They jointly formed the "Christopher Reeve Paralysis Foundation", raising money and awareness for spinal cord injury research and raising the hopes of thousands of paralysis victims throughout the world. She carried on as president of the foundation after Chris' death.

I had the honor of writing Dana's biography for Wikipedia. The more I researched her life, the more I admired her. Politically, we were polar opposites — she was an avid liberal and actively campaigned for John Kerry. But I have to admit, she was my favorite liberal. I always dreamed of meeting her in person some day.

Last year, she was diagnosed with lung cancer, although she had never smoked a day in her life. Throughout her treatment, she maintained a rigorous schedule of public appearances in support of the Foundation. Publicly, she said that the cancer was responding to treatment.

She died last night, leaving behind a son, 13-year-old William. She'll be missed.

She was 44.

Kirby Puckett was 45.

I am 49.

Living in the Past

A couple of years ago, a co-worker told me that I was living in the past. When I asked her to explain she said "You're always talking about the way things used to be. You're always bringing up stuff that happened years ago."

Well, she was kinda right. She saw it as a flaw. But I see it as my need to gain perspective.

That's why I enjoy studying sappy lyrics and 70s songs and stuff like that. That's how I anchor myself. I find something that appeals to me and I latch on to it. Maybe I take it to an extreme sometimes, but I don't think so. I think what I'm really doing is finding what works for me and then sticking with it. There's nothing wrong with that. It beats wandering around aimlessly, looking for a purpose in life.

One of my favorite teachers in school was my seventh grade social studies teacher. One day, at the beginning of the school year, he wanted to impress on our junior high skulls of mush the importance of studying history. So he called me to the front of the class and told me to walk across the front of the classroom, but to do it walking backwards. After I did it, he asked me how I did it. It took a little prodding — I didn't understand what he was getting at — but the lesson was that the only way you can walk backwards is by watching the path where you've been. You don't have eyes in the back of your head so you can't actually see where you're going. But if you study where you've been, you'll always have a clue of what's coming up next. It's not perfect — but it's all you've got.

And that's how life is. You have no choice — you *have* to walk through life backwards. You can never see what's coming next. But if you never lose sight of where you've been — if you study your past and the consequences of going through it — you'll have at least a glimpse of what's yet to come.

And that's a lesson that I still remember 35 years later.

I Don't Watch Television

The Academy Awards were presented last night. Don't expect to find out from here who won. I have no idea.

I can say (with just a little bit of pride) that I have not seen any of the movies that were nominated for any major Academy Award this year. None. I saw lots of movies last year, but none of the nominated ones.

That really isn't remarkable. Oscar finally jumped the shark in its snobbishness this year and didn't nominate a single blockbuster movie from the previous year. Very few people have seen any of the nominated movies this year. So I guess I'm in good company.

But I have other distinctions that I apparently don't share with many Americans. I don't watch much television, either.

I am one of the few people on the planet who has never seen an episode of "Friends". Never. I've seen a couple of Jennifer Aniston movies, however. She *was* on that TV show, wasn't she? I dunno. Is it still even on?

I saw only two episodes of "Seinfeld" while it was on. And one of those was the series finale.

I may have watched a couple of episodes of "Cheers". I can't remember. And I think Kelsey Grammer went on to star in something else after that, didn't he?

I've heard that there are a dozen different shows on TV named "CSI" or some other TLA.

I have never seen an episode of "Survivor". But last spring a friend convinced me to get hooked on "American Idol". I probably saw two-thirds of the episodes, but I missed the finale when Carrie won. I yawned.

I own a television and I subscribe to basic cable. TiVo has no interest for me. I watch a lot of Fox News, some Discovery Channel and Court TV. My son is hooked on Nickelodeon.

But me? If it's a series — if it's fiction — I have no use for it. The truth is strange enough for me.

What If You Don't Agree With Me?

Sometimes I'll post things to this forum that not everybody agrees with. Some people write to me and say they don't agree with me. They have very strong, convincing arguments that prove their point. And they demand that I post a retraction to this obvious erosion of the truth.

The simplistic response to them would be that they have every right to be wrong. After all, I wouldn't have posted it if I hadn't believed in all my heart that I was telling the truth. Actually, it's more than that — it's not just that I *believe* I am posting the truth. In fact, *it is* the truth. After all, how can truth be relative?

But that goes beyond the stated purpose of the forum. It's not my intent to prove that I'm right and you're wrong — however true that might be. My intent is to drill a hole in my head, insert a microscope, and invite you to peek inside.

If you discover *why* I believe the things that I do — whether you agree with me or not — then the stated purpose of the forum has been fulfilled.

On the other hand, if you walk away from here thinking "How can he be such an idiot..." — well, you have a right to be wrong.

A Lesson in Accountability

A few days ago, I learned a lesson in accountability. My eight-year-old son had to use my computer to look for pictures of invertebrates on Google and Wikipedia It was for a science notebook that he's working on for school.

My browser has an auto fill-in feature, which means that if he typed in something that was close to something I had already typed it, it would try to complete it for him. That means he pretty much has access to everything that I have ever looked up.

I look up a lot of stuff on Google and Wikipedia. Some of it is because of my job. Some of it is related to research that I'm doing for other projects I'm working on. And some of it is just because I'm naturally curious. I never look at anything on the Internet that I wouldn't want my son to know about.

But it was a reminder to me that he's getting to the age where he's going to want to use the Internet to answer questions that he might not want to find out anywhere else. It was a nice reminder to me that he's watching everything I do, which is a heavy burden for me to bear.

Speaking of stuff that you find on the Internet... Did you know that Samuel Seymour was the last person alive to actually be present when Abraham Lincoln was assassinated? He was five years old and was in Ford's Theatre attending "Our American Cousin" when he heard the shot and saw all the commotion. He appeared on the TV game show "I've Got A Secret" in 1956, just a couple of months before his death at age 96. (His secret, of course, was that he had witnessed Lincoln's assassination.)

The things you learn on the Internet...

Erratic Mouses and Other Problems

Here's something that's amusing and frustrating at the same time:

My computer was having an erratic mouse problem. The pointer would slow down, would crawl, would leap all over the screen as if it had a mind of its own.

While trying to fix the problem, one of the things that I tried was to download a new mouse driver from microsoft.com. That didn't help any, so I un-installed the driver. That didn't help, either, but I was finally able to fix it the problem doing some other stuff.

I later stumbled on to some other entries on Microsoft's web site that dealt with erratic mouse behavior.

One said the symptom was "a slowing of the computer and erratic mouse behavior". So I dug further. The cause listed was "recently installed mouse driver downloaded from microsoft.com".

Their solution? *Un-install the driver!*

So on one page, they say that the problem can be fixed by downloading and installing this driver. On anther page, they say that the problem may have been caused because you followed their advice on the previous page to fix the problem that you started out with. And their solution is to un-do the solution that they previously told you about to fix the problem that their solution caused!

Sheesh... talk about circular logic!

If that story made you alternately shake your head in disbelief and nod your head in wise agreement, you're just geeky enough to be my kindred spirit.

And all you Mac people out there — I don't want to hear from you. You've got enough other problems.

Two Things Corporations Don't Do

Gasoline prices are currently at or near all time highs. It really doesn't matter when you're reading this. The fact is that virtually everything that you purchase is currently at its all time high. It's called inflation. It's a natural by-product of capitalism and is nothing to be feared. Get used to it.

Nevertheless, it seems that petroleum prices have gone beyond the natural bounds of inflation, so people are looking for an enemy to blame.

It's easy to blame oil companies. So oil companies are currently out of favor. They tend to rotate with the pharmaceutical companies, insurance companies, Microsoft, and Wal-Mart. At any given point in time, at least one of those will be in the dog house with consumers. Today it's the oil companies. In a couple of months, one of the others will take over the bad-guy slot and oil companies can go back to business as usual.

Since we're always blaming big business for everything from droughts in the Sahara to floods in the Midwest, maybe it's time to have a quick lesson in economics. The following are two basic truths of big business. Don't argue with me. You know I'm right:

Corporations don't make profits

Corporations don't pay taxes

I have yet to meet a liberal that understands these concepts. At least none that would admit it in public. Because if they would be honest and admit that these are true, they would have to reconsider every shred of public policy that they've worked so hard to establish in the last fifty years.

What do you really think happens when corporations make profits? Do you think it just goes into the pockets of the fat-cat executives? Well, yeah, some of it does. And I suppose you could make arguments as to the appropriateness of that. But even if the highest paid executive would distribute his entire year's salary to all his customers, it wouldn't put any more than a couple of bucks in your pocket. Executives make a lot of money because there are a lot of customers out there.

The dirty little secret that liberals don't want to admit is that virtually all corporate profits go back to the shareholders. And *we* are the shareholders. You and me.

Much, if not most, of the public stock of large corporations is held by mutual funds and retirement accounts. IRA's. 401k's. You can rejoice when a corporation announces record profits because a lot of that money is going to be paying helping you put gas in your Winnebago in a few years. When corporations make money, we all make money.

Liberals would have you believe that it's not fair when corporations make so much money. So they would rather impose insane "windfall" taxes on corporations. They have this crazy notion that they can tax corporations and nobody will notice it. They never met a tax they didn't like, and they especially like the ones that they believe "nobody" pays.

Of course, they forget that corporations don't pay taxes. It's just part of doing business. It's figured into the cost to the consumer. Sometimes the consumer actually “sees” it, as in the case of his utility bill or telecommunications bill. But most of the time it’s just baked into the cost.

Every time I read that some huge corporation has just received some big tax break, I say hurray, because I just put more money in my pocket. And when I hear that they have reported record profits, I say hurray again, because I put even more money in my pocket.

I thank them, my retirement fund thanks them, and some day my Winnebago will thank them.

The Question My Dad Wouldn't Answer

To an eight-year-old boy, Dad is perfect. He has no faults. Dad is on the highest pedestal in the land. He never makes mistakes. He never sins. He's never wrong. He is, after all, Dad.

Dads get a lot dumber, of course, as the boy enters his teen years. But to an eight-year-old, Dad is perfection personified.

I know, because my dad was perfect. Even when he didn't know the answer, Dad always had the right response. And that's what I'm going to talk about today.

We were watching a movie on television that was not originally filmed in English. It was French or German or Japanese or something. Whatever. It wasn't English. But it had been "dubbed" into English.

Even as a small boy, I understood the concept of dubbing. I knew that they originally filmed the movie in some language and then later some actors went into a sound studio and recorded their voices in another language to match the expression and tempo and dialog of the original actors as good as possible. It wasn't an exact science, but it was certainly serviceable.

As Dad and I watched the movie together, it occurred to me that they had to get rid of the original dialog somehow. But there were all these other sounds in the movie. There was music. There were ambient sounds in the outdoor scenes; birds chirping, cars whizzing by, feet shuffling on the sidewalk.

How, I asked Dad, did they remove the dialog without affecting all the other sounds in the movie? I'll never forget his reply.

"It ain't easy."

In other words, he didn't know.

I accepted that as an eight-year-old. I accepted the fact that he didn't know, but he wasn't quite ready to admit that he didn't know. But that was okay. Because Dad was perfect.

Over the years, I've had some experience in the recording and video production industries and now I know how they did it.

You wanna know?

When a movie is made, the sound is recorded in layers. The music is always recorded on a completely separate track. Usually the dialog is on a track by itself. As much as possible, the sound is recorded completely "dry", without any ambient noises at all. No footsteps, no doors squeaking, no fingers rattling on computer keyboards. Those sounds are added later by "foley artists" — very similar to the "sound effects" actors in the old days of radio drama.

All these individual tracks are blended together to create the final product that we enjoy as a movie. But they are also kept separate so individual tracks — such as the original dialog — can be removed and new dialog inserted.

In those occasions where it is impossible to separate the sound effects from the dialog, it is possible to recreate the sound effects on the foley stage along with the new dialog. It can be done so seamlessly that it's barely noticeable.

So, there you have it, Dad. That's how they do it. I thought you'd like to know.

And by the way, if you didn't know it before, your secret's safe with me.

All Energy is Solar

We've been hearing a lot lately about alternative energy. I gained a better understanding of energy when I came to the realization that all energy comes from the Sun.

No matter what kind of energy you consider on the Earth, it all originated with the Sun. Petroleum started out as organic material, grown by the Sun. Hydroelectric power wouldn't be possible without the sun's role in evaporation and condensation. Even wind energy is the result of the sun's uneven heating of the planet as it rotates on its axis.

All energy is solar.

If all energy came from the Sun, where did the Sun get its energy? Well, the Sun is basically nothing more than hydrogen and helium. The Sun keeps these two elements in a constant state of nuclear fusion, giving off vast amounts of energy and generating more energy in a few seconds than we could ever use in our entire lifetime.

All energy is nuclear.

But what sets off such fusion? After all, hydrogen and helium are the two lightest elements in the universe. How can they get together to create energy? They do it by simple mass. The Sun is so big that by its sheer gravity, these tiny elements are held together and compressed to a point of fusion. If it wasn't for gravity, the electrons and protons would simply float aimlessly in space.

All energy comes from gravity.

Gravity is one of the greatest mysteries of the universe. Nobody understands what forces are at work that draws two masses together. But it's universal. Every mass attracts every other mass. It is that attraction that creates the energy that we get from the Sun. Yet nobody can explain.

Well, I can explain it. God is pushing things together. There can't be any other explanation. If you can't see the power of God's creation in the structure of a flower or in the engineering of the human eye, surely you have to admit that the only explanation for such a force is that gravity is the Hand of God.

All energy comes from God.

A Price for Everything

A basic axiom of capitalism is that everything has a price. Any product or service — regardless of its moral or ethical value — can be one side of a transaction in which the other side is money. The amount of money exchanged represents a point somewhere between the value of *obtaining* the product or service to the purchaser and the value of *delivering* the product or service to the seller.

An economics teacher once postulated this to his class in this manner: How many people in his class would be willing to have the tip of their little finger cut off? The class was understandably squeamish at the prospect, so he elaborated.

The tip of the little finger would be surgically removed at the first joint. There would be no pain and no ill effects from the surgery. The only thing is that the person would have to live with the inconvenience of missing the tip of their finger for the rest of their life.

Okay, given that, how many people would accept that offer?

No hands were raised.

Okay, let's sweeten the pot. What if they were to be paid one dollar? Would that make a difference?

Again, no takers. So he doubled the ante. Two dollars for cutting off the tip of your little finger.

Nope. Nobody would do it.

Five hundred dollars? A few people in the room squirmed nervously.

Okay. *Ten million dollars.*

Every hand in the room shot up.

So the fair market price of cutting off one's finger is somewhere between five hundred dollars and ten million dollars. The only thing left to do would be to work from both ends until the final price is agreed upon.

That's how auctions work. That's how eBay works. Heck, that's how capitalism works. It's a wonderful system. And, just like abstinence, it works every time it's tried.

This is nothing new. One of the most enduring examples is in the world's oldest profession. And it was wonderfully illustrated in Julia Roberts' breakthrough movie, "Pretty Woman".

Julie Roberts and Richard Gere negotiated her fee for a week's worth of service. The auction takes only a few seconds — a few lines of the movie. Finally, they settle on $3,000.

Once they shake on the deal, she confesses, "I would have stayed for two thousand." He replies, "I would have paid four."

So the fair market price of a week with Julia Roberts at your beck and call is somewhere between $2,000 and $4,000.

Nah, that was in 1990. The price has probably gone up since then.

Midnight on Television

There's nothing like comparing youthful memories of television with some young 30-something whipper-snapper to remind me exactly how old I am.

I recently discovered that some of my co-workers didn't realize that TV stations used to play the Star-Spangled Banner every night at midnight. Why would they do that? That's silly.

These kids grew up with MTV and fifty 24-hour cable channels. Now they have 200 satellite channels but they hardly ever watch any of them live because they TiVO everything. In other words, they have no idea what it was like to watch television in the 1960s.

Forgive me for a few minutes while I address such uninformed citizens and teach them about television at its finest.

When I was growing up, we could receive three television stations. Just three. One for each network. Yes, there were only three networks back then: CBS, NBC, and ABC. That is, if you could really consider ABC a network.

The evening news came on at 10:00. For the next half-hour, we were treated to a summary of the entire day's world news in the first 10 minutes. Then there was a smattering of local news. After a commercial, we learned about what the weather was going to be tomorrow. Then 10 minutes of sports, which usually meant finding out whether the Cardinals won or lost that day.

What happened after that depended on what channel you were watching. If it was the NBC channel, you saw an hour and a half of The Tonight Show Starring Johnny Carson. If you were watching the CBS channel, it may have been an old movie or some rerun or something. Nobody knows what you watched if you were watching the ABC channel, and nobody cared.

That means that all the stations ran out of programming somewhere around midnight. They were done for the day. Some sleepy engineer hung around to make sure the transmitter was still humming. But the news crew had all gone home by then and all the front office guys had left a long time ago.

So when the last minute of programming was done, it was somebody's job at the TV station to play the Star-Spangled Banner. It was usually a tape of a choir singing — Mormon Tabernacle-style. Or it may have actually been the Mormon Tabernacle Choir. I dunno. Or it may have been a military band. Whatever. And it was usually accompanied by a film of a waving American flag.

And then there was an awkward silence. A test pattern may have come on for a few minutes. And then a pop. And then snow.

Then the engineer turned out the lights, locked the door, and went home. About six hours later, the day shift engineer would show up to broadcast the morning farm reports. On NBC stations, that was followed by The Today Show. On CBS stations, it was followed by Captain Kangaroo. Nobody knows what was on the ABC stations because nobody watched them.

What is "snow", you ask? That's what we called the electronic blizzard that filled the screen accompanied with white noise. I know most of you people under 40 have never seen static on a TV screen. Well, that's the stuff you get when you send a TV signal over the airwaves and it bounces off of the local water tower and you get a ghost image and...

No, no, TV doesn't have to come over a cable. You could actually get a TV signal from the atmosphere. I mean without a dish. It didn't come from outer space; it came from a tall, skinny tower that is usually visible from the interstate. But you needed an antenna as large as your kitchen table which looked like a bunch of coat-hangers that fell out of the sky into a symmetrical triangular pattern.

This is all very confusing for you, isn't it?

Wait until I tell you about the days when CDs were twelve-inches wide. And black.

Conservative Activism vs. Liberal Activism

Every once in a while, I listen to liberal talk radio on Air America. From what I've been able to figure out, whenever I listen, the total audience of Air America increases by about 20%. (They're being beat by Caribbean Music formats.) And based on listening to the callers to their shows, I have determined that when I listen, the intelligence of their audience quadruples.

I love studying the difference between conservatives and liberals — especially the different ways they approach activism. That was illustrated recently when I listened to Air America's coverage of recent Minutemen activities.

The Minutemen Project is a group of citizens along the US-Mexico border determined to monitor the flow of illegal aliens and report their activities to US Border Patrol authorities. They recently discussed a proposal to help local citizens erect their own fence along the border if the US government refuses to erect such a fence.

The Air America hosts ridiculed the plan as the world's easiest fence to "walk around". In doing so, they demonstrated that they have no idea how conservatives view activism.

To a liberal, activism is chaining yourself to a tree. Or putting a flower in the barrel of a soldier's gun. Or marching down the street. All these activities are designed to convince *somebody else* to solve *your* problem. After all, it's never a liberal's fault that a problem exists, so a liberal never actually believes that he can solve the problem. That's what the federal government is for.

But to a conservative, activism means actually *doing* something to solve the problem. And that's what the Minutemen activists are doing. While the liberals are running all over the country wringing their hands, convincing Congress to change law-breaking free-loading aliens into legal free-loading citizens with the stroke of the legislative pen, the Minutemen are actually on the border solving the problem at the source. They are proving that where the federal government is inept, private citizens will be effective.

And that brings us to the fence.

The Minutemen have long supported the building of a heavily-patrolled fence along the US-Mexico border. From the Pacific to the Gulf. Through desert and along the river. Makes sense to me. Most countries have to build fences to keep their own people in. It's not that we want to keep people out, but we need to control the flow of people as they enter. And it's kinda hard to do that if they can just walk in after supper and show up at our schools knowing only three words of English: "Free lunch program".

The Minutemen have enlisted a dozen or so landowners along the border that have agreed to build the fence on their land. Of course, building the fence on disjunct land won't be totally effective unless the fence is built along all 2,000 miles of the border. Thus, the ridicule by the Air America hosts.

But they're missing the point. The Minutemen are setting out to prove that such a fence can be built. It can be built by private enterprise using private money. In the areas that it exists, it can be 100% effective. The federal government has the money and the resources to build such a fence. The Minutemen are demonstrating that if the federal government won't build the fence, it'll get built anyway.

They're actually *solving* the problem.

No war was ever stopped by putting a flower in the barrel of a gun. But our county may be just a little more secure with some strategically placed barbed wire.

Great Scott! I Coulda Been Great. Like Scott.

Scott Adams, the creator of the Dilbert franchise, and I have a lot in common. We're both about the same age. He used to work at a large telecommunications company in the West. I work for a large telecommunications company in the Midwest.

We both share a healthy cynicism of large corporations, although his is directed at the entire company whereas mine is usually focused on the IT department.

We are both software engineers who took the MBA route into business.

For many years, he kept his day job while writing Dilbert on his kitchen table late at night and early in the morning. I have kept my day job while I write this blog late at night and early in the morning.

Scott has made millions of dollars from people that clamber to read the words he has written. I ... still work at a large telecommunications company in the Midwest.

My path actually crossed with Scott's once several years ago. I wonder if he remembers me. He had asked his fans to send in stupid things that we had heard our boss say. I sent him a list of, gosh, twenty or thirty stupid things I had heard bosses say. It wasn't hard coming up with the list. My favorite: "It's not that kind of zero." Don't ask the context; it can stand on its own.

In a few days, I got a nice email from Scott saying that he was going to use my quote in his next newsletter. Sure enough, a couple of weeks later, there it was. I was in print. Well, actually, a millionaire had just used my contribution for free to make some more money. I figure he earned about $15.37 by copy-and-pasting my words. Actually, my boss's words. Hmmm... I wonder if I owe my boss a commission. I'll pay him when Scott pays me.

Scott owns one of the world's most famous email addresses: scottadams@aol.com. He regularly published that email address in the Dilbert comics years before it was fashionable to even *have* email addresses. Heck, a lot of people probably didn't even know what an email address was at the time. Of course, now most people have a dozen or so addresses. And scottadams@aol.com probably gets ten thousand spam messages a day.

Dilbert was the first comic that actually understood technology. While Dagwood was still making sandwiches and Dolly was still "touching" Jeffy, Scott actually mentioned the term "control-alt-delete" in one of his earliest comics. I'm sure several editors got letters complaining that the comic was too out-of-touch for common folk. He was giga-years ahead of his time.

So Scott has his millions and I have my credit cards. Scott can stay in the finest hotels in the world and I drive miles down the interstate looking for the nearest Super 8. Scott's books, comics, and blogs are read by millions and my blog is read by my mother — when I print it for her and put it under her nose.

Scott and Dilbert are featured in no fewer than a dozen Wikipedia articles. But I can lay claim to one bit of notoriety that Scott will never be able to surpass. I wrote the Wikipedia article about Manhattan State Hospital, the hospital that Scott Joplin died in. Really.

Hah! Top that, Mr. Adams. You may be able to become wealthy drawing a guy with no mouth. But I can write an article that nobody reads about a hospital that doesn't exist anymore that once counted as its patients the greatest rag-time composer of all time.

Well, everybody's gotta start somewhere.

Fire Alarms are Serious Stuff

We had a fire alarm at work today. Well, it wasn't really an *alarm*, it was a *false* alarm. That meant it was really more of a drill.

I work in a big office building with a few thousand other people. It's actually like a small city. It's larger than the town I grew up in.

The standard protocol when the alarm goes off is that everybody is supposed to put down whatever they're doing and calmly walk toward the exits. Don't take the elevator on the way down; that would be bad luck. Then we are supposed to congregate in the parking garage across the street and walk around aimlessly until we notice that people are streaming back into the building because, after all, there never was any fire in the first place.

I've added a few rules of my own. For one thing, I always take my car keys. And my laptop computer. And I get one last good drink of coffee. (You never know when you're going to get your next one.)

It's hard to take these things seriously. If I would hear a big bang or actually see smoke some place, I'd probably be more anxious to get out the door. But as it is, I usually take my time to look around my desk to see if I'm forgetting anything.

We get these things every couple of months or so. They are almost always false alarms. Usually, it's not a fire; it's just some maintenance worker standing on a ladder with his head poked into a drop-down ceiling saying to himself, "Hmmm, I wonder where *this* wire goes to?" Then "snip" and "tweet-tweet-tweet".

My first clue today was the attitude of the maintenance people I saw on my way out. I noticed several of them congregating around the alarm command center. Laughing. Oh, well. The rules say to get everybody out of the building first and ask questions later.

Actually, I don't mind. The very first fire "drill" in this company that I was involved with was a real fire. Really. It happened several years ago, but it changed the way I look at fire alarms.

A bunch of us were working on the 14th floor when the lights dimmed. Then all our computers re-booted. There was a collective "ugh" that went through the office as everybody realized that their work was lost. Then the whole floor went dark. The emergency lights came on. And a few seconds later, the fire alarm sounded.

The guy I was working with asked me if this was a drill. I said "I dunno, but I'm not going to hang around to find out."

The stairwell was crammed, but we were all orderly. Concerned, but civil, as we walked down 14 flights.

We all congregated at the base of the building. After a while, we learned that there had been a fire in the main electrical transformer that fed the building. We were not in any danger, but it was going to be many hours before it was going to be fixed so we could all go home.

So I headed for my car. And then I realized where my car keys were. On the 14th floor. And all the elevators were dead.

Two lessons I learned that day: Take every fire drill seriously. Always remember your car keys.

My knees ached as I walked up the fourteen flights. They ached more as I walked back down.

Many years later, two airplanes crashed into the buildings of the World Trade Center. In the few minutes that followed there was a lot of confusion about whether or not to evacuate the buildings. Many people jammed the stairwells going down while others wandered aimlessly wondering what to do. The irony was that the people watching it unfold on the TV news knew better what was going on than the people in the building.

Thousands of lives were saved that day by people that knew to treat every alarm seriously. Get out of the building and ask questions later. Hundreds more may have been saved if everybody had taken that advice.

My guess is that at the end of the day, the last thing that was on everybody's mind was whether they had remembered their car keys.

In Real Life, Clowns Aren't Always Sent In

Remember the song "Send in the Clowns"? Judy Collins popularized it in 1975, although it was originally written a couple of years earlier by Stephen Sondheim for the musical "A Little Night Music".

Like many songs of the era, the true meaning behind the lyrics is somewhat esoteric. It appears that the singer is going through some hard times, trying to figure out the disappointments of life in general and relationships in particular. Then this "Send in the clowns" line pops up. What's with that?

Here's a reminder of the first verse:

==============================

Send In The Clowns
Words & Music by Stephen Sondheim

Isn't it rich? Aren't we a pair?
Me here at last on the ground, and you in mid-air.
Send in the clowns.
Isn't it bliss? Don't you approve?
One who keeps tearing around, and one who can't move.
But where are the clowns? Send in the clowns.

==============================

Allow me to explain about the clowns.

In any live performance, sometimes "stuff" happens. When it happens on Broadway, that usually means somebody forgot their line. Or a dancer has a sprained ankle. Or the tuba player has asthma.

But when "stuff" happens in the circus, it may mean that somebody just fell off the high-wire and is now laying in two pieces in the middle of ring number two. Or some trapeze artist ate too much buttered popcorn and his slick fingers failed to catch his partner. Or somebody got his head bit off. Literally.

Who cares about asthmatic musicians when performers are dying?

In the tradition of "the show must go on", well, the show must go on. The traditional response by the circus management is to send the clowns in to entertain and distract the audience while the maintenance crew mops up the mess in the dark, leaving the audience to wonder if that was really all part of the act.

When tragedy strikes the circus, the cry goes out backstage: "Send in the clowns!" And everybody knows exactly what that means.

Sometimes life is like that. Sometimes things get so bent out of shape that you find yourself looking around for the clowns. Surely there must be some comic relief around here. Surely. Somewhere.

But not always. Here's the last verse:

Isn't it rich? Isn't it queer,
Losing my timing this late in my career?
But where are the clowns?
There ought to be clowns...
Well, maybe next year.

The clowns don't always show up. Sometimes there is no comic relief.

Sometimes you just have to face your problems with no help. Either that, or find your own clowns. Because this ain't the circus.

This. Next. When? What?

Today is Monday the 17th. What will be the date next Friday?

Okay, show of hands. How many people said the 21st? How many people said the 28th?

You wanna start a big argument over something that should really be simple? Throw that question out at the next lunch table and see what your co-workers say.

People have been dealing with the concept of relative time for several millennia. But they have yet to figure out what to do with the word "next". The problem comes when people confuse "next Friday" with "the Friday in next week".

If you have no idea what I'm talking about, you would say the answer is the 21st. If you're saying to yourself, "What does he mean? They're both the same thing!", you would say the answer is the 28th.

See the problem?

There's a very simple solution to the proper usage of the word "next" when dealing with relative dates.

Don't use it. Never. Kinda like the word "bling". Don't try to use it in a sentence. It's too ambiguous, too confusing, and totally unnecessary.

Here's the real answer. (Remember, you heard it here first.)

This Friday is the 21st. *A week from this Friday* is the 28th. *Next* Friday is undefined, just like dividing by zero. It just doesn't exist.

See? Nothing hard about that.

Nobody is ever confused about “this”. It’s always the next one coming up. It’s the word “next” that they have a hard time with. But once you’ve established what “this” is, it’s only a small step to define “a week from this”.

No ambiguity. No confusion.

Sheesh, do I have to explain *everything* to you people?

Watching the Girl from Ipanema

I love people watching. I love to sit in the mall and just watch the world go by. There is something about knowing that you are "in" on a tiny sliver of a person's life as they walk by that can be downright exhilarating at times.

Of course, when the subject is "people" watching, it invariably turns into a discussion on "girl" watching. And for a very good reason.

Men use the act of walking to get from point "A" to point "B". It's nothing more than that to them. They are not trying to communicate anything. They are just moving their carbon-based molecules through space.

Women, on the other hand, often feel like transportation — pedal or otherwise — is a statement. (Not all women believe this all the time, but enough do to make it interesting.)

Women treat walking as a three-step process. They get ready for it, they do it, and then they admire their accomplishment.

Whereas men simply move through space, women actually take over and occupy the space for a brief moment. After a woman has walked by, it is natural to stop and take a poll — ask the audience what they thought of the message that the woman left behind. To do so after a man walked by would be an exercise in futility.

If you've done as much girl watching as I have, you will notice that women are naturally divided into two categories: the attractive women and the not-attractive women. Don't argue with me on this one; you know I'm right.

I have also noticed that the attractive women tend to naturally fall into two sub-categories: those who are aware of their attractiveness and those who are unaware of it.

It is that last group that intrigues me the most: the attractive women who are unaware. They are the most innocent, the most alluring. They go through life making a statement, but they don't even know what that statement is. As they pass men, the men acknowledge that they are a beauty to behold but are the same time untouchable. For unless a woman is aware of the effect she is having, it would be a sin to take advantage of it.

Whenever I think of girl watching, I have to think of music. It's only natural. Heck, Herb Alpert & the Tijuana Brass had a hit song on that very subject — "Music to Watch Girls Go By".

But it is another song that epitomizes the very essence of girl watching. It's one of the most recorded songs in the history of music — the one that introduced the rhythms of the bossa nova to much of the world.

================================

The Girl from Ipanema
Music by Antonio Carlos Jobim
Original Portuguese lyrics by Vinicius de Moraes
English lyrics by Norman Gimbel

Tall and tan and young and lovely

The girl from Ipanema goes walking
And when she passes
Each one she passes goes "aah"

When she walks she's like a samba
That swings so cool and sways so gently
That when she passes
Each one she passes goes "aah"
================================

Now *there* is a beautiful girl who has absolutely no clue the effect she has on the men as she passes them.

Ahhhhh.

Just Vote "No"

When politicians run for office, they have to beg for votes. Most constituents won't vote for a candidate unless they're actually *asked* to vote for them. And *buying* votes is generally frowned upon in our society.

So here comes Mr. Candidate to Mr. Voter and he says, "Will you vote for me?" What's the first thing that Mr. Voter is going to say?

"What are you going to *do* for me?"

I suppose that's a legitimate question. The problem is that politicians generally can't really do much for their constituents.

Except spend money. Your money. *My money.*

And how do they spend it? By voting. Specifically, by voting "Yes".

At this point, I should pause and say that most of this is directed at the federal level. The closer politicians actually get to the voters, the less this is true. I'd really like my city councilmen to continue to spend money to fix the potholes on my street. But I'm just about at the point where I don't want my congressmen and senators to spend any money at all except on federal defense.

And the best way to measure how well they do that is to see how often they vote "No".

Political organizations have been rating politicians for years based on how they vote. Most of these organizations track how politicians vote on specific issues of concern to them. A "Yes" vote or a

"No" vote could be for or against that particular organization's agenda.

I'd like to see a different view. I'd like to know how many times a politician voted "Yes" or "No" regardless of what the issue is.

I know there are some issues in which I'd like to see a "Yes" vote. But every "Yes" vote involves spending some money, even if it's money that I wouldn't mind them spending. The only cost for a "No" vote is the electricity to light and air-condition the chamber while the vote is occurring. I'd be willing to pay for that.

Imagine this. A candidate seeking a political position says something like this in his "stump" speech: "If you elect me, I promise that I will save more of your money than my opponent and I will not spend one dime more than what is absolutely necessary to guarantee the security of our country. I will do this by voting 'No' more often than any of my colleagues in Congress."

That's the guy who would get my vote.

Trickle-down Works in France, Too

When I was a poor, struggling college student, I got a job one summer working for a small factory on the edge of town. It was such a small factory, I was working with the owner.

I spent two weeks loading and unloading bags of cement and other construction materials into trucks. It was hot, hard, back-breaking work.

At the end of the two weeks, the owner of the company reached into his back pocket, withdrew two weeks' salary in cash, thanked me for my time, and said I wouldn't be needed on Monday.

I was disappointed. Even though I had been hired very casually, I kinda thought the job was mine for the summer. But, no, he just needed me to get through a busy part of the season and my services were no longer needed.

I was grateful for the work, thanked him for the opportunity, and went out looking for my next job — which I found a few days later. That job — in a local truck stop — lasted me through the end of the summer.

It's a good thing I didn't live in France. Otherwise, I wouldn't have had a job all summer.

America's unemployment rate usually hovers around 5%. France's is now in the low 20% range. But that's not good enough. The youth of France will not be happy until they have achieved a full 100% unemployment rate. With the help of French namby-for-president Jacques Chirac, they are well on their way to just that.

France seems to have a law that says that once you've hired somebody, it's really, really hard to get rid of him. You can't just say, as the factory did to me, I'm sorry, we have no more work for you to do.

No, you're stuck with him.

When the French government tried to amend the law this spring to give just a little more flexibility to employers, the youth of France did what they've been doing since the 17th century. They revolted. And the leadership of France did what they've been doing at least since World War II. They caved.

Socialists gain power by claiming to represent the working class — usually at the expense of business. They have never realized that what is good for business is usually also good for the workers. And what is bad for business is invariably bad for the workers.

Trickle-down economics — like gravity — doesn't have to be believed in to work.

Policies that are repressive to business — like minimum wage laws, guaranteed employment laws, and employee-financed health care — always look good on the outside but will almost always backfire in the face of the very people they are trying to help.

Thankfully, guaranteed employment laws didn't exist in America when I was in college. If they had, those trucks would have never gotten unloaded.

This Forger Got Away with It

One of this year's most amazing stories involves a forger who recreated one of America's most famous and iconoclastic paintings. And when the forgery was discovered, the official reaction was, "Well, that is certainly interesting."

Here's how it happened.

In the 1970s, Donald Trachte was best known as an illustrator of the famous "Henry" comic strip. That bald, speechless boy had been a classic in American newspapers since 1932. Trachte had been drawing the character with John Liney ever since the original creator, Carl Anderson, had died in 1948.

Trachte was also a good friend and neighbor of the great American artist, Norman Rockwell. When he wanted to buy one of Rockwell's paintings for his private collection, he was offered *Breaking Home Ties*, for which he paid $900 in 1960.

This was one of Rockwell's greatest paintings. Appearing on the cover of *The Saturday Evening Post* in 1954, it depicted a young man ready to leave for college, accompanied by his farmer father. The elder, hat in hand, is contemplating his future and perhaps offering a last piece of advice as the son anxiously awaits the bus that is going to take him to school. They are both sitting on the running board of a beat-up pickup truck. A faithful collie rests his chin on the boy's knee.

It can easily be said that Trachte got a bargain. Art critics often rated *Breaking Home Ties* as one of Rockwell's greatest paintings, in the same vein as

Rosie the Riveter, which was sold for $5 million in 2002. Paying $900 for a multi-million dollar painting was a good deal.

Trachte proudly displayed the painting as the centerpiece of his private collection right up until his death last year.

And all along, he was displaying a forgery.

For reasons unknown, Trachte himself painted an exact copy of the great picture almost as soon as he bought it. It was the *copy* that he had displayed all these years. And it was such a good copy — such a perfect copy — that nobody noticed the difference.

Nobody did, that is, until this year when the family discovered the painting — the real painting — hiding behind a wall in his house where Trachte had stashed it thirty years ago.

Nobody knows why he made and displayed the copy. It certainly wasn't for financial gain. It couldn't have been for security; the original was no more secure behind the wall than the copy was hanging in public.

Whatever the reason, it died with the forger. And no hard feelings are present, either. The plan is to display both the original and the forgery side-by-side in the Norman Rockwell Museum in Stockbridge, Massachusetts.

Be sure to listen to Paul Harvey's *The Rest of the Story* in the next few weeks. My guess is that this remarkable story will be featured.

And you can tell your friends that you heard it here first.

The Right-Sizing of Self-Service

When the retail industry was in its infancy, self-service was non-existent. You told the clerk in Sam Drucker's General Store (usually Sam himself) what you needed and he went around the store and fetched it for you. You went to a shoe store, picked out the style of shoe that you wanted, and a man in a suit went through a curtain to the back room or climbed a ladder that was on wheels and brought your shoes to you in your size. He even wedged them on your feet for you.

If you went to the lumber yard or hardware store for nails, there was always somebody there to scrape your nails from a bin, weigh them carefully, and put them in a brown paper bag for you.

If you needed to buy gas, driving over a black rubber hose was the signal to the mechanic that he had a customer. He would put down the wrench (where he had been changing the spark plugs or a fan belt on somebody else's car), wipe his hands on a greasy red rag, and come out to your car. You stayed in the car while he pumped your gas, checked your oil, and cleaned your windows. If you were paying by gas credit card (virtually the only thing bought on credit those days), he would take your card inside, run it through the machine, and bring out a receipt for you to sign on a specially designed clipboard. You kept the carbon copy (a real *carbon* copy). The receipt was usually smudged with grease from his hands.

Retail has now turned almost completely upside down. Store associates are there only to stock shelves and take your money. Sometimes they don't even do that.

At many stores, you scan and bag your own purchases. Shoes are usually bought off the rack. And almost nobody will pump your gas any more.

Retailers have discovered that they can save a few bucks by making the customer do some of the work. And customers have decided that they like the lower prices and increased flexibility of self-service. So it looks like a good match.

But here's the paradox: Even as we enter a more *self-service* society, the largest growing sector of employment is the *service* industry. Even as we are charged less for doing somebody else's work, we are paying more to have other people do *our* work.

We pay people to raise our children. We eat out more often, so we pay people to cook many of our meals. We pay people to clean our carpets, mow our lawns, and walk our dogs.

When I make pancakes, it used to be that I added oil and eggs to a pancake mix. Now I only have to add water to the mix I buy. Not only am I paying somebody to pre-mix the flour for me, I'm paying somebody to add dehydrated eggs and oil, too. (Dehydrated oil? Well, you get the idea.)

Heck, when I have Eggo's for breakfast, I even pay somebody to cook them for me. All I have to do is pop them in the toaster.

It's called the "Right-Sizing of Self-Service". In areas where it makes sense, the consumer has taken over services that were previously done by professionals. And in other areas where it makes sense, consumers have allowed new professionals to take over. And we are willing to pay them a premium for doing so. Everybody wins when such adjustments in society are made.

This is best exemplified by studying what happens when I buy gas at my favorite convenience store. I am willing to get out of the car and stand outside in the weather to pump my own gas, wash my own windshield, and swipe my own credit card.

When I'm done, I go inside and pay them $1.50 to fix me a cup of coffee that I could have brewed at home for a nickel.

Everybody wins. The store gets more profit because they hired me to pump my own gas. And the store gets more profit because they just sold a new product to me at a 10,000% markup. I'm happy because my hands now smell like petroleum products and I get to spill hot coffee on my pants at the next stop light.

A free-market economy — like all forces of nature — tends to correct itself in the long run. And just like nature, it works best when it's left alone.

Health Insurance, Not Health Care

A recent article in the Kansas City Star spotlighted doctors who work outside the safe confines of the insurance industry. When you visit one of these doctors, you either pay for the service they provide or they send you a bill. The patient is free to either pay the bill or file the charge with his insurance company for payment reimbursement. According to the article, approximately 10% of all doctors in America operate with such a policy.

Imagine that. Paying for a service that is provided directly to you. *What a concept!*

It's not an original idea. The entire health care industry operated like that until somewhere around the middle of the last century. Then somebody got the bright idea that employers should pay for health care.

Where did that come from? Does my employer pay for my gasoline? Does my employer buy my eggs and milk and bread? Does my employer pay my rent or my mortgage?

Then why should I expect my employer to pay for my health care?

What's worse, common thought is now trying to make my *government* pay for my health care. Yeah, just like my government pays for my eggs and milk and bread and housing. I don't think so.

The state of Massachusetts is trying to circumvent the issue. They recently passed a law that *requires* all citizens to buy health insurance. Remember, any time a government says you have to pay something, it's really a tax — no matter what they call it. So the State of Massachusetts has just achieved the distinction of being the first state in 100 years to attempt to enforce a poll tax. That indeed is what it would be: *a tax on living*. If you live here, you pay this.

The problem comes when people confuse health *care* with health *insurance.* I want to treat health insurance like car insurance. When I need an oil change or a new set of tires or new wiper blades, I buy them. When a large, unexpected expense occurs — like a major accident — my auto insurance is there to help me pay for it.

Did you get that? *It's insurance, not care.*

Some people bristle at the thought of paying for their own health care. The dirty little secret is *you are already paying for it.* Health care benefits are currently paid from insurance premiums and taxes, which you paid in the first place. Why should I pay an insurance company to pay my doctor? I'd rather just pay him in the first place and take the insurance company out of the picture completely.

I'll keep my health insurance as a cushion against large, unexpected health care costs. Other than that, I'd rather just pay my doctor in the first place. That's the best way I know of reining-in spiraling health care costs.

Why the Poor Are Poor

Jackson County, Missouri, which contains most of the Kansas City metropolitan area, recently held an election to determine if a three-eighths cent sales tax should be imposed to pay for improvements to the local sports stadiums. Ostensibly, it was implied that the NFL Chiefs and the MLB Royals would bolt for more profitable venues if the tax did not pass.

Voters approved the tax by a slim 53% margin. The stadiums will be upgraded and the major league teams will be ensconced for at least 25 years.

Over the last few months, the debate had centered on the wisdom of a county imposing a sales tax on those who are arguable the poorest in the metropolitan area. (Rich suburban Johnson County made it clear that they were not going to be any help.) After all, a sales tax is one of the most regressive means of tax collection available. The poor pay a proportionally higher portion of their disposable income on sales taxes. Why should they bear the brunt of subsidizing rich franchise owners as they put on a show to entertain rich business owners and their rich clients in their rich luxury boxes?

Why, indeed? Good question. So it would make sense that *poor* people would not be in favor of this, because they'd be the ones paying for other peoples' pleasures. Right?

Nope, that's not the way it turned out. The maps printed in the Kansas City Star reveal the truth. As a whole, the county was almost evenly split on the issue. But it failed overwhelmingly in the rural, suburban, and affluent sections of town. And it *passed* overwhelmingly in the inner-city core.

That's right. The *poorest of the poor* are the ones who *want to be taxed the most* so other people can benefit.

From what I can figure, the liberal mindset that made most of the people poor in the first place has as its core the belief that the government should take money from people because it knows how to spend it better than the population as a whole. And the philosophy that made them poor is the philosophy that will keep them voting for policies that will guarantee their poverty in perpetuity.

The Bible tells us that the poor will always be with us. The modern day axiom is that the poor get poorer because all they know how to do is to repeat the actions that got them there in the first place. And the rich will get richer because, well, all they know how to do is to repeat the actions that got them there in the first place.

It kinda reminds me of the advice that I once heard on learning how to run: "Place one foot in front of the other. Repeat vigorously."

It works every time it's tried.

Cosmic Dust and Other Saturnian Stuff

The Cassini spacecraft, currently in orbit around Saturn, is solving one of the oldest mysteries about Saturn's rings.

It has long been believed that the rings are the result of collisions of various solar system objects. But one thing has puzzled scientists for years. If the rings are actually made of pieces of collided matter, there should be a wide variety of sizes of matter. Until recently, only dust-like particles have been observed.

Think of it this way: Drop your favorite piece of fine china on a marble floor. Go ahead, drop it.

Okay, just *remember* the last time you dropped your favorite piece of fine china. What did you get? Two or three large pieces, a dozen or so smaller pieces, some small chips, and some pieces that were reduced to dust.

Physicists tell us that whenever matter separates or coalesces, it will form a few large pieces, several medium-size pieces, and millions of tiny pieces. And what happens in your kitchen happens on a cosmic scale as well.

Back to Saturn's rings. If the rings were formed by a collision, where are the larger pieces? Last year, Cassini found a few small "moonlets" inside the gaps between the rings, right where the theory said they should have been.

And last week, it was announced that several medium particles were discovered plowing a path through the rings. Finally, all three sizes of particles have been observed. Physics once again was proven by superior engineering.

What happens on your kitchen floor and what happens in the sub-system of Saturn happens in the solar system at large, too. There are a couple of large planets — Jupiter and Saturn — several medium planets — Earth, Venus, Mars — and millions of tiny planetoids — asteroids, the Kupier belt and a bunch of other stuff whizzing around out there. We've even discovered a tenth planet outside the orbit of Pluto. And we've found a few other planet "candidates" around the orbit of Neptune.

And remember all the glass "dust" on your kitchen floor? The solar system is full of it. The weight of the Earth actually increases by thousands of tons every year as it accumulates dust in its orbit. You see this on dark nights as shooting stars.

So here we are on our medium-size planet, zipping through space, accumulating dust, surrounded by stuff of all sizes. The solar system used to be such a "neat" place; nine planets and few asteroids. We are now beginning to understand just how incredibly complex it is. Just like that fine china on our floor.

Here's a Frog with His Head on Straight

I always liked Kermit the Frog's song "It's Not Easy Bein' Green", written by Joe Rapposo. I never realized until I studied the lyrics how much it lacked meter, form, and any real semblance of poetry. It's really like a bunch of mumbling that Kermit is doing to himself while letting us listen in.

But there is a lesson to be learned in that mumbling. Listen with me:

He starts with a basic premise:

> It's not easy being green, having to spend each day the color of the leaves. When I think it could be nicer being red, or yellow or gold — or something much more colorful like that.

I'll have to agree, of all the colors I might want to be, green would not be one of them. It brings about images of Mr. Spock's blood.

Kermit continues:

> It's not easy being green. It seems you blend in with so many other ordinary things. And people tend to pass you over 'cause you're not standing out like flashy sparkles in the water — or stars in the sky.

Ah, that's the real issue. Kermit doesn't think he's ugly. He thinks he's *unspectacular*. He thinks he's unnoticeable. And he's right. That's why frogs are green; to blend in. But Kermit is not your normal, everyday frog. He doesn't want to blend in.

One of the greatest fears of man is that he will go through his entire life and not be noticed. That's why politicians worry so much about leaving a "legacy". They want to know that they made a difference. Everybody deserves to be told that, at the end of their life, they made a difference. Nobody wants to be "green" if it means leading a life of irrelevance.

Then Kermit's thoughts take a turn.

> But green's the color of Spring! And green can be cool and friendly-like. And green can be big like an ocean, or important like a mountain, or tall like a tree.

If on the surface, green is irrelevant, Kermit realizes that it doesn't *have* to be. There are a lot of great things that are green — mountains, oceans, trees. And they aren't irrelevant. It's kinda hard to miss a mountain.

> When green is all there is to be it could make you wonder why, but why wonder why? I am green and it'll do fine. It's beautiful! And I think it's what I want to be.

Yup, Kermit is happy being green. But he's happy because that's what he's decided to be.

It isn't easy being green. But you can make it work. It's your choice.

It's the Details

Actors learn lines. Actors speak lines. Actors remember their blocking. And they remember to always face downstage. But then, so do cartoon characters. True thespians, on the other hand, spend the first *five minutes of their career* doing that. The rest of the time is spent working on the details. It's all about the details.

When I was a budding, young, high school thespian, a theater major from the local college came to our drama class to give a miniature seminar on acting.

We were all in high school and he was still in college. I remember thinking, *What can he possibly know? He's, what, five years older than us? What can he have learned in five short years of drama training that we don't already know?*

Yeah, like most high school students, I was an arrogant brat who figured I already knew it all. Here was this college "hippie" that was going to teach me how to act.

Actually, he taught me a lesson that I still remember 35 years later.

He had just completed his school's production of *You're a Good Man, Charlie Brown*. He played Snoopy. *Oh, great, he knows how to play a dog. I, on the other hand, had just played the lead in* Our Town. *Top that, college boy!*

I remember he talked a lot about the difficulty in playing a part that could talk to the audience, but could only communicate in gestures to the other cast members. That meant every gesture — every movement — had to have meaning. The audience was going to be noticing and interpreting everything he did. *Everything.*

I listened a little closer.

He spent ten minutes talking about one scene. No, he spent ten minutes talking about one *part* of one scene. He spent ten minutes talking about *30 seconds of acting*. This was a guy that appreciated detail.

In this scene, he had to complete a "conversation" with Charlie Brown and then defiantly walk off stage. Stage left; I remember it well. And in the process, he had to direct the audience's attention away from Charlie Brown, toward himself, and then toward his exit, and then across the stage and into the wings.

Everything he did had a purpose. His eye contact with Charlie Brown. How he raised his hand. How he literally threw his arm across his body in the other direction. How he twirled his head. How he directed his attention off-stage. Everything.

This was a guy that knew the importance of details. That short lesson affected the way I have evaluated theater ever since.

Many years later, I watched an interview of an actor from one of my favorite shows: Michael J. Fox from *Family Ties*. He talked about his favorite episode, a "coming-of-age" episode in which his 18-year-old character got into an argument with his mother, played by Meredith Baxter-Birney. It was a typical son-feels-trapped-by-his-parents, mom-can't-let-her-baby-go script.

When Fox talked about filming the show, did he talk about how he got through it without missing any lines? Did he talk about how he could make his co-star giggle? Did he talk about blocking or camera angles or lighting or makeup?

No. He talked about *electricity*. The episode was filmed before a live audience, which always gives sit-coms a sense of “presence”, of “real-ness”. He talked about how he engaged the entire audience in the argument. He made everybody believe that this was a real son arguing with his real mother about real issues.

He created real electricity by paying attention to the details.

For a more current lesson in details, watch Reese Witherspoon’s performance as Elle in *Legally Blonde*. In one classic scene, she appears in a Playboy bunny suit at a party that she thought was supposed to be a costume party. She holds her head up high and gamely makes it through the evening. But then she has a confrontation with her boy friend and suddenly realizes that he cares much more about his friends than he does about her.

In a single camera shot, the color drains from her beautiful face. We see her go from happy to hurt in a few short seconds. Her smile disappears, her eyes sadden, her shoulders droop ever so slightly. She matures twenty years right in front of us.

No wonder many have proclaimed Reese to be the successor to Julia Roberts. She knows how to pay attention to the details.

Political Traffic

I'm one of the only people in the world that can take an issue like freeway traffic design and turn it into a political issue. Watch how I do it.

My recent business travels have taken me to a couple of cities where the freeways have HOV (or "high-occupancy vehicle") lanes. Sometimes they're called "diamond" lanes. The idea is that there has to be at least two people in the car to drive in the lane. Yeah, that's "high" occupancy. Two people.

The intent is to encourage carpooling. Maybe if we can get more people to share rides to work, we'd have fewer cars on the road polluting our air, filling our atmosphere with ozone, and melting those ice caps.

The problem is they don't work.

HOV lanes do virtually nothing to change people's behavior. If you're going to carpool, you're going to carpool. If you're not, you're not. The prospect of saving a few minutes on the ride to work isn't usually worth the extra time it takes waiting for Dagwood to plow into the mailman on his way out the door.

So HOV lanes reward people for practicing the behavior that they would be doing anyway. They get to shave a few minutes off their commute just because they happen to have a friend riding shotgun. Oh, and sometimes that "friend" is an inflatable guy named "Irv" whose only purpose is to thwart the system and scare car-jackers.

And at what cost? Well, it makes sense that if one lane is less-traveled and going fast, the other lanes are more crowded and going slower. Yep, HOV lanes not only reward the unworthy, they punish people just for trying to get to work on time.

Wouldn't it make more sense to evenly distribute the traffic amongst all the lanes and give everybody a fair shot at a pleasant driving experience?

Which leads me to my political discussion. I have noticed that HOV lanes appear primarily in cites with a predominant liberal bent. This is a rather unscientific observation, but it makes sense. HOV lanes demonstrate exactly what liberals typically do. They attempt (and fail) to legislate behavior while giving the appearance of rewarding that behavior. The chief benefactors are people who don't deserve to be rewarded. Although most people experience a reduced level of service, the authorities can pat themselves on the back for giving the appearance of doing something worthwhile.

I'm familiar with at least one city that has a different approach. Dallas has express lanes that let you fly past the stalled traffic. For a price. It costs something like a quarter or something to enter these lanes. Kinda like a toll road parallel to the main road. You can decide whether the improved experience is worth the cost.

What a concept! Making people pay for a rewarding experience and then giving them a proven benefit as a result.

Oh, yeah, Dallas is one of the most conservative cities that I'm aware of.

Conservatism. Works every time it's tried.

Slaves to Fashion

Every year about this time, women's fashion turns inside out, upside down, and just about every way except the one that makes sense. You start seeing parts of their bodies that you don't normally see. Like their ankles sticking out from beneath their pants.

They're called capris; pants that are almost long enough, but not quite. When I was growing up, "high-water" pants were any pants that didn't quite meet the top of your shoe. And it wasn't meant to be a compliment.

In the early 1960s, Laura Petrie delighted men with her amazingly-tight, painted-on capris. The culture of the time wasn't quite ready for explicit displays of sexuality, but the producers of the show saw that young Mary Tyler Moore had assets that they couldn't afford to ignore. So capri pants became popular, women showed their ankles, and men smiled.

Men are still smiling, but not because they are seeing women's ankles. That's old news. Seeing women's body parts is no big thrill any more. But watching women being total slaves to fashion is still a hoot.

Capri pants left us after the Dick Van Dyke show went off the air, but they reappeared on the scene in the late 1990s. And for only one good reason: fashion designers — mostly men — love to mess with women's minds.

The fashion mavens have convinced women that they need two completely distinct sets of wardrobe;

one for winter and one for summer. It has nothing to do with the weather or with comfort. Rather, it concerns arcane rules like not wearing white after Memorial Day. Or before Labor Day. Or something like that. I can't keep it straight.

Men like me have it easy. I have only a couple of fashion decisions to make every day. If I'm not going to work, it's blue jeans. If I'm going to work, it's not. Other than that, short sleeves or long sleeves. That's not hard.

Before my company went to that oxymoron called "business casual", the decision was basically my gray suit or my *other* gray suit. Well, it really wasn't a decision, I just rotated them. Luckily, I had two suits and there are five days in each week, so it wasn't like I wore the same suit every Monday or whatever. (Think about it.)

My ties were in a similar rotation. After all, every tie goes with a gray suit and white shirt.

But women. Poor women. They have suits and pants and dresses and skirts and sweaters and shirts and blouses and shoes and shoes and shoes. And tops. I never have figured out what a "top" is. Isn't it a blouse? Or a shirt? Why does it need its own name?

And double that list because winter pants can't be worn in the summer. And summer pants show ankles and we can't have that in February, can we? And tops may be sleeveless, but only a few months every year.

And sweaters aren't built to keep women warm; their purpose has something to do with showing curves or hiding curves or something like that. But not in the summer. No, during that time they are moth food in some drawer somewhere.

I'm glad I'm a guy. I show my ankles only when I'm not wearing socks, which is usually only in the bathtub. Nobody tells me what to wear or when. I can wear the same shirt on Christmas or on the Fourth of July. My shoes are practical and functional, not fashionable.

And my "tops" are never sleeveless. For that, you should be eternally grateful.

My Favorite Wedding Song

My nephew got married last week and I had the honor of providing the piano music for the wedding.

This wedding, like most, could be pretty much summed up in a few key points: The bride was beautiful, the groom was clueless, and the father of the groom (in this case, my brother) was totally irrelevant.

When preparing music for a wedding, I usually work exclusively with the bride. After all, besides the obvious, the groom has only two jobs: Say "Yes, Dear" and "Where do I sign?" If it wasn't for those two duties, the groom would be as irrelevant as his father.

A bride usually has a few songs in mind that she definitely wants included in the ceremony. I'm expected to "fill in the gaps", based on my standard wedding repertoire.

This wedding followed that script exactly. The newest-member-of-our-family-to-be had a couple of songs that she wanted me to play. Beyond that, I was all on my own. Just the way I like it.

The reason I like it so much is because it allows me to "sneak" in a couple of my favorites — songs that the bride would probably never have requested, but that I like. And keeping the musician happy is part of any good performance.

Given my absolute and total distain for country music, it is ironic that my all-time favorite wedding song is (I cringe to say this) a county ballad. The way

I play it, it sounds more like it came from Barry Manilow or Lionel Richie. But it was actually first made famous by Lee Greenwood.

================================

I.O.U.
by Austin Roberts and Kerry Chater

You believe that I've changed your life forever
And you're never gonna find another somebody like me.
And you wish you had more than just a lifetime to give back all
I've given you; and that's what you believe.

But I owe you the sunlight in the morning
And the nights of all this loving that time can't take away.
And I owe you more than life, now more than ever.
I know that it's the sweetest debt I'll ever have to pay.

I'm amazed when you say it's me you live for.
You know that when I'm holding you you're right where you belong.
And, my love, I can't help but smile with wonder
When you tell me all I've done for you,
'cause I've known all along.

But I owe you the sunlight in the morning
And thc nights of all this loving that timc can't takc away.
And I owe you more than life now, more than ever.

I know that it's the sweetest debt I'll ever have to pay.
================================

If every groom would read these lyrics to his new bride on the night of their wedding, the world would be a much better place.

One partner may enter a relationship thinking that the other has done everything to give their life more meaning. But a great relationship begins when one realizes that they go into the partnership owing the other so much more.

It's a debt they'll never be able to repay. But should spend the rest of their life trying.

On Being from Missouri

I have lived in Missouri my entire life. That gives me the right to say some things about Missouri that people who don't lived here can't say.

Just because I live here, that doesn't make me a "Missourian". In fact, there is no such thing as a "Missourian". We aren't really *from* here. We just happened to *live* here.

I've always admired people who live in Oklahoma, Texas, or California because they can proudly and rightfully say that they are Okies or Texans or Californians. There is a distinct culture behind those words. People know exactly who they are and what they stand for.

Being from Missouri, however, simply means that I live in Missouri. In has no significance beyond that. There is no defining culture that we can associate with.

Missouri isn't simply a diverse state; it's a downright *fragmented* one. There are two large cities: St. Louis and Kansas City. People from St. Louis don't like the people from Kansas City. People from Kansas City don't like the people from St. Louis. People who live in neither city don't like *anybody* who lives in a city.

Well, I'll take that back. Everybody has an allegiance to one of the big city's sports teams. Somewhere down the middle of the state — probably right along Highway 63 — there is a line that separates the Royals fans from the Cardinals fans.

And it separates the Chiefs fans from the Cardinals fans. I mean, the Rams fans. Whatever.

Another line of demarcation is the Missouri River. It splits the state in the other direction. There are mountains to the south (if the Ozarks can be called "mountains") and there *aren't* mountains to the north. Nobody from north of the river likes anybody from south of the river. And the people south of the river don't care.

The city names in Missouri are funny, too. Did you already notice that one of the largest cities is actually named for a rival *state?* Who's idea was that? Oh, well. Half of Kansas City is in Kansas, anyway.

Even though the largest cities are St. Louis and Kansas City, neither of them is the capital. That honor goes to — anybody? — that's right, Jefferson City. Who woulda thought? It was named after the president that bought the state from the French. (The name "Missouriopolis" was first proposed for it. In a rare move, wiser heads prevailed.) It has the distinction of being one of the few state capitals that isn't served by an interstate highway. Now, *there's* an honor that needs to be passed around.

Other cities are named for other states, too. It's like they just couldn't be original. There's both a California and a Florida in Missouri. And there's a Nevada, too. Except that they pronounce it Nuh-VAY-duh. Nobody knows why.

Some cities were named after exotic places like Paris and Versailles. (Don't even ask how they pronounce that.) They just couldn't think of anything better to name them.

Heck sometimes they'd just give up naming cities. Halfway is, well, half way between Buffalo and Bolivar. Ten Mile is ten miles from Macon. They might as well have named them "We're almost there".

We haven't had our fair share of famous people originate from Missouri. Well, there was Mark Twain. But he didn't want anyone to know who he was, so he didn't use his real name. When he wrote his famous books, the non-anthropomorphic star wasn't the town in Missouri, it was the river — *the river that is named after another state!* Sheesh.

Oh, yeah, and Harry Truman was from Missouri. Of course, he was a failed businessman who was used by the political machinery of the time to become a senator. Then he accidentally stumbled into the presidency. He was barely re-elected once and then he saw the handwriting on the wall and decided to get out while the getting was good. He was replaced by a Jayhawk from Kansas.

It's hard being from Missouri. Easterners call it "flyover country". Westerners think we're somewhere near Pennsylvania. Northerners think we're a Confederate state. Southerners call us Yankees.

Of course, I can say things like that about my state, but you can't. After all, *I am a Missourian.* Whatever that is.

Soaps in Perspective

A recent interview with actress Kelly Monaco provided an interesting view of the unique perspective enjoyed by television daytime dramas ("Soap Operas", to the uninitiated).

Miss Monaco said she hoped her win in last summer's "Dancing with the Stars" reality show would provide more interest in daytime dramas. (Her "day" job is playing con woman Sam McCall on "General Hospital".) She expressed that desire after noting that daytime television has "kind of fallen off a bit ... ever since the O.J. Simpson trial."

Honey, that trial was ten years ago. And you're just now noticing it?

Kelly's confusion can be excused, considering she has spent the last six years in the fantasy world of the tube. Such is how things move on soap operas. They broadcast five hours a week with hundreds of pages of dialog in each show. But the plot moves at glacial speed. And that's being generous.

I admit that when I was fresh from college and teaching in public school, I got hooked on "The Young and the Restless". Since I generally had the summers off with little to do, I got involved in the lives of Lorie, Leslie, Lance, and Lucas as they bounced their affections amongst each other. It was a harmless diversion. And the neat thing was that I could occasionally skip an episode and never miss anything.

Being a school teacher, I had a week off during Christmas. What had happened while I was gone?

Not much. Usually by Tuesday, I had filled in all the gaps. I swear that sometimes I would leave Lorie and Lance in the middle of a discussion in late August and they were just wrapping up their little chat in December.

We usually had a snow day or two in January and February. That let me keep up with things. When June rolled around, I was back at it. Except now it was Lorie & Lance and Leslie & Lucas instead of Lorie & Lucas and Leslie & Lance. You get the idea.

A few days ago, I had to get my car repaired. While waiting in the "customer service" room at the dealership, the television was tuned to — you guessed it — "Y&R". (It is now hip to identify soaps by their initials. I dunno, I guess it saves electrons in cyberspace or something.)

Well, the four L's are now gone. But wait. I recognize ... could it be? Yes! Victor and Nikki. Gosh, I hadn't seen them in years. They were rather minor characters during the LoorieLancyLukeyLeslie era of the show. But, yeah, I remember them.

Turns out they've been there all this time. Gosh, 25 years or so. I think during that time they've each been married seven or eight times. To each other a couple of times. But they keep plodding along in one of the most-coveted gigs in the entire acting industry.

In the episode I watched, they were carrying on a discussion that I think they started last October. It had something to do with somebody's baby who had amnesia and who looked a lot like the character that they had killed off a couple of seasons ago during a contract dispute. Victor said something profound. The camera zoomed in on a close-up of Nikki's face to capture her reaction shot for, oh, about twenty seconds. It must have been a slow dialog day.

Then they went to a disposable diaper commercial followed by a tile cleaner commercial and another for some woman's product that I didn't fully understand.

Then I heard the announcement that my car was ready.

I think I'll catch up with them at my next oil change to see if Nikki's face is unfrozen.

Being a Great Employee

I have written a bunch of performance reviews in my life. I've hired a lot of people and have written reviews on them. I have written reviews on myself so my boss could claim ownership of the review while relieving him the stress of actually making a judgment on somebody else's performance. And, through the miracle of "360" evaluations, I've had a chance to write performance reviews on my boss. (Those are usually a hoot.)

When I am asked for my philosophy on what makes a good employee, it is easy for me to narrow my thoughts down to two guiding principles. When these principles become the driving force of an employee's work ethic, the employee is virtually guaranteed a stellar review and success in business beyond all imagination.

1. Make your customer happy.
2. Make your boss look good.

That wasn't hard, was it? But that's how simple it is. To look good at work, the secret is to unselfishly help those around you.

I have never worked in any retail environment in my life. Not once have I actually had to deal with the public. When I refer to customers, mine are always "internal" customers — people who work in the same company with me but that I do work on behalf of. But I suspect that the same principles hold true even with the more traditional definition of "customer".

Notice that I stop short of saying "the customer is always right". We all know that in many cases, the customer really doesn't know what's best for him. After all, that's why we're providing the service, right? So the secret isn't to always do exactly what the customer tells you to do. Success occurs when the customer is "happy". That way he'll pay his bill on time, leave with a smile on his face, and tell all his friends what a wonderful experience he just had.

If the customer isn't "right", that's okay; you just have to figure out some way to make him see the error of his ways. And make him think it was *his* idea — that's the tricky part. A customer who has just been sold the "wrong" product won't be happy, even if it was his idea. But a customer who believes he changed him mind of his own free will — and only because it makes sense — that's a customer that will keep coming back for more.

Regarding the second principle, keeping your boss happy. Now that Scott Adams has appeared on the business books scene, it is finally fashionable to say out loud what we've all know for ages: bosses are clueless. Sadly, they kinda enjoy it. There's really no reason to interrupt their ignorant bliss. But the fact is, they somewhat control our destiny. They have the power to hire and fire, they give and deny raises and promotions, and they provide for our general well-being. So what are we to do?

It's not enough to make them happy. The funny thing about our bosses is that they are actually smarter than our customers. So they can't be duped into believing that changing their mind is a good idea, whether it's their idea or not.

But the one thing they do understand is recognition of their successes. They love to be praised for good work — whether they actually did the work or not. They have fragile egos that must be constantly stroked. (Most of them are men, after all.)

So your job as a good employee is to make sure that your boss is in a constant state of looking good to his boss and his peers. Your boss must look like the hero. Your boss must be the one who saved the company, who invented the perfect product, who raised revenue and cut expenses with one blow. You do the work, he gets the credit, and I can guarantee you, everybody will be happy.

Lay your selfishness aside; there is no place for it in business. Not when you could have pure greed instead. It's much more rewarding. And it can be yours if your customers are happy and your boss looks good.

My Commencement Address

One fantasy that I have had my entire life is that just once I would love to give the commencement address to the graduating class of a high school or college. It wouldn't have to be a big school. A few dozen mortarboards in front of me would be fine.

I've done plenty of public speaking in my life, but it's mostly been corporate presentations or training or some sort of church teaching. What I really want to do is face a group of skulls of mush who think that they know everything and impart upon them my half-century of wisdom. I figure I'd have plenty to say.

Actress Jodie Foster recently got her chance when she gave the commencement address to graduates at the University of Pennsylvania in Philadelphia. I'm not sure exactly what her credentials were that got her the gig. Well, okay, she did graduate twenty years ago from rival school Yale. I guess I can't say that. My MBA from a prestigious private school and my stellar career in marketing makes for a good résumé, but not much star power.

Oh, and she's got four Oscar nominations and two wins. That beats my recent victory in the Pinewood Derby at church.

Of course, any Hollywood type with a penchant for left-wing activism can't be satisfied with merely reminding graduates that this is the first day of the rest of their life. Or that a journey of a thousand miles begins with a single step. No, she was obliged to insult the very country that gave her the right to speak to the graduates in the first place. And she didn't disappoint us in that regard.

She told the graduates that the county is worse off than it was four years ago. Regardless of who is in power, when either side uses the term "four years ago", it is euphemistic for bashing the President. So a free Iraq, lower taxes, a booming stock market, and virtually no unemployment are all Bush's fault.

She also ragged on the administration for the "disastrous and shameful" handling of Hurricane Katrina. Hey, lady. I was there. The place was a mess. You think you could've done better? Anyway, both the mayor and the governor are Democrats. There's plenty of blame to go around.

Okay, I'll cut her some slack. After all, she graduated from an Ivy League school.

If I had been in front of that audience (or any appreciative audience, for that matter), I could have summed up my entire speech in three words: "Never stop learning."

Well, maybe four words: "Never *ever* stop learning."

Don't ever think that you know it all. You're just beginning. You haven't learned anything yet. You've just learned *how* to learn.

School doesn't teach you anything. It teaches you how to organize your life. It teaches you how to do research. It teaches you how to figure things out for yourself. Then you spend the rest of your life doing just that.

When I interview people for a job, I rarely care what kind of degree they have. I only care that they finished something. You don't learn stuff for my job in college. But I need to know that the people I hire know how to learn. And *want* to learn.

They need to display to me an insatiable desire to do better. To figure things out for themselves. Not just to think "outside the box", but to figure out how to build a box and then build a better one.

There. That's my graduation speech. Now I've just got to wait for my phone to ring from some Ivy League college president wanting me to say the same things to his graduates.

But why should I? They could just come here and read it for themselves.

Faking It

Just about anything that can be manufactured can be faked. Money. Drivers licenses. Designer jeans. Even conversation.

A couple of weeks ago, a friend of mine told me that he had to hurry home to watch that evening's episode of "American Idol".

I acted unimpressed. "The chick's gonna win," I offered.

"I dunno," he replied. "I think that skinny guy's got a pretty good chance.

I smiled. Once again I had proven to myself that any conversation can be faked, even if you know absolutely nothing about the subject.

I hadn't watched an episode of "American Idol" all year. I have absolutely no interest in the topic at all. I read an article in Reader's Digest about last year's winner and I had seen enough in the papers to know that most of the time a chick is usually one of the last ones standing. So I figured it was a safe bet to lead any discussion about the show with "The chick's gonna win." Can't fail.

I live about half of my life making conversation about things I have absolutely no knowledge of or interest in. I'm one of those guys who knows just a little bit about a lot of things but not a lot about anything. So it's relatively easy to find some common ground, run with it, and then just follow the lead of the other person.

When the topic turns to sports, it's almost always possible to say something like "Hey, how about that game last Sunday?" It doesn't matter that you don't know who played on Sunday. The chances are that *somebody* played. Once you figure out who played and whether they won or lost and if the game ended on a controversial play, the rest is easy.

This is possible because of two tendencies of human nature. One is that people will always fill in the blanks in their own mind. That's why pixilation works. People can see that digital pictures on a computer screen or in a magazine are really just a series of dots. But their minds fill in the gaps between the dots to make a continuous picture. They do the same thing in conversation. When presented with incomplete facts, people fill in the unknown facts with facts of their own choosing. That's why you don't have to say the name of the chick that's going to win or the name of the team that played last Sunday. Given an incomplete thought, people will instinctively fill it in.

The other bit of human nature that makes it work is that people tend to advertise their thoughts. It's called "telegraphing". Poker players learned this a hundred years ago. They don't know if their opponent has a good hand by reading the back of the cards. They can tell a lot more by reading their eyebrows and the corners of their mouth.

Mind-reading magicians — they like to be called "mentalists" — have made a living of doing this. A common trick it to get an audience participant to reveal secrets without realizing it. A mentalist may ask a widow, "Did your husband linger before he died or did he pass quickly?" When the widow replies that his death was very quick, the magician can say, "Yes, I thought so, because I hear him telling me that there was no pain." She goes away amazed that the guy actually talked to her dead husband.

Most of my friends don't know how many conversations I fake, but my guess is that it's three or four a day. It's not really deception, sometimes it's just the polite thing to do. I'd rather spare them the embarrassment of telling them that I'm really not even remotely interested in their trivial drivel. I've kept a lot of friends by being dishonest with them.

Besides, it's kinda fun.

Continuity Goofs

Every movie fan knows that films are full of continuity errors. These are little inconsistencies from one shot to the next within the same scene that are usually blamed on somebody not paying attention in the editing room.

Meg Ryan's sandwich reappears after having been eaten in "When Harry Met Sally". Hugh Grant's tie changes patterns in "Love Actually". And Julia Roberts' croissant magically turns into a pancake in mid-sentence in "Pretty Woman".

Some people delight in spotting these subtle nuances of movie-making. The "goofs" section of IMDB.COM is full of user-contributed tidbits. Sometimes it seems that people spot these things just so they can say, "Aha! Gotcha with another error!" They can't wait to email their brother-in-law with a new discovery.

Famous writer-actor-director Garry Marshall lets us in on a little secret about continuity goofs. Many times, they are included in the final cut of the movie for a very good reason: To make the actors look good.

Each scene in a movie is usually shot multiple times. They are shot from every conceivable angle. From above, from below, from the left side, from the right side. Sometimes that's done to move equipment out of the picture. Sometimes it's done to create an illusion of three dimensions on the set. Sometimes it's done to create alternate dialog or alternate plot lines that may be selected from later.

And many times, it's because directors know that actors are human.

To maintain a sense of spontaneity in dialog, movies aren't always rehearsed as thoroughly as theatre productions. The actors are often creating their mannerisms and nuances of dialog literally on the spot. In one take they may raise an eyebrow or emphasize a syllable differently. They may look down or up or away at a particular moment. Those are the subtle little things that audiences see but never notice. But they're the things that make a movie believable. The director is constantly looking for them.

In the editing room, a director will pick the best takes in each scene and cut them together to create a seamless stream of dialog. And that's where Mr. Marshall is willing to fall on the sword for his actors.

When a continuity error is discovered, nobody blames the actors. It's always the director's fault or the film editor's fault. But if an expression isn't right, if a line is slightly mis-delivered, if the "magic" isn't there, the actors take the heat.

As a director, Marshall would rather be blamed for a continuity goof than have his actors look bad. So he always takes the very best performance. If somebody's hair style doesn't quite match up from one camera angle to another or if a water glass is full after having been drunk, so be it. The actor's performance is the sole determining factor in selecting a take for a particular shot.

In Marshall's movies, the director's job is to make the actor look good. The result is a great movie with believable action.

And if it adds a few more bullets to the "goofs" section at IMDB, then at least somebody's brother-in-law is happy.

How I Eat

It's a good thing that I never took up smoking. If I had, I'd be one of those guys that has about five different lit cigarettes in various stages of being smoked spread around in every ash tray of the house.

That's assuming of course, that I would smoke with the same degree of self control that I exhibit when I eat snacks. And I think there is enough similarity between the two habits that that's not a long stretch to make.

I often buy bags of potato chips from the vending machine and bring them back to my desk at work. Three minutes later, I absent-mindedly reach for another chip and discover — horror of horrors — the bag is empty.

And I don't remember eating a single chip beyond the very first one.

My right hand is a venerable feeding machine. And my mouth is a most gracious receiving trough. The act is completely automatic and instinctive. It doesn't matter if I'm actually hungry. If there is food within two feet of my right hand, it is scooped up and deposited into my stomach.

I used to work with a woman who had the exact opposite tendency. She was a tiny waif of a creature, and her eating habits matched her stature.

One time, a salesman brought a box of chocolates to me in the office so I decided to share them with my co-workers. I stopped at her desk and offered her a piece. Why yes, she graciously looked over the variety and picked one with the appropriate swirl.

Then she set it down on her desk next to her keyboard, smiled at me, and *went back to work*.

I almost fainted from the shock.

Waitaminnit! Don't you understand? This is a piece of candy. A piece of *chocolate* candy. It is designed specifically to be taken from the box and placed between your teeth. You don't make a masterpiece like that wait until you're in the mood to nibble on it. You *devour* it. Then you look for the next one. And you repeat until the box is empty.

No thanks, she smiled. She'll eat it later.

There was no reasoning with her.

Of course, this was the same 90-pound weakling that bought a bag of M&Ms from the vending machine, sorted them by color, and lined them up on her desk to eat them one at a time. One "M" every ten or fifteen minutes.

She could make a three-minute bag last all week.

I may not have the most health-conscious eating habits in the world. But at least I appreciate the value of good, quality vending machine food. I only wish I could make it last longer.

The Paradox of Digital Data Eternity

Man has dreamed of eternally preserving data for, well, forever. The ancient Egyptians thought they had done a pretty good job of doing that by drawing on the walls of tombs buried in the desert. Until everybody forgot how to read hieroglyphics. Thank goodness for that Rosetta Stone thing.

The Romans assumed that their empire and their language would exist forever. Their language is kept alive in state mottos, but not much else.

In the twentieth century, we invented methods of converting all data into digital formats. And that, we thought, solved the problem. Not only could we preserve data for all eternity, we could effortlessly and precisely transmit that data instantly over virtually unlimited distances. And we could replicate that data over and over and over again with absolutely no loss in quality from the original to the ten millionth copy with a precision that those 12th century monks would surely be envious of.

Alas, it didn't occur to us that the very technology that would make that possible would soon be replaced by — *better* technology. Sheesh. Who woulda thunk that?

You have seen this problem if you have ever tried to recover that résumé that you "preserved" five years ago on a 3.5-inch floppy disk. Heck, most the computers today don't even have a slot to plug that thing in any more. I worked for a company that had shelves of data sitting on eight-inch floppies. That was back when floppies actually *flopped.* That data might as well be sitting at the bottom of the ocean today.

The Census Department discovered the problem in the 1980s when they realized they could not read data from the 1960 census. It all existed on magnetic tapes that could only be read by tape drives that didn't even exist any more. They spent $10 million dollars figuring out a solution to fix the problem.

NASA had a slightly different problem. It had acres of data from the early lunar explorations that it could read, but it couldn't make any sense out of it. The documentation and original file structures had been lost and the men who worked on those projects had mostly retired. They had to pull a bunch of their old engineers off the golf courses to come in and make sense of the mess.

Since technology outpaces technology at an ever-alarming rate, this is not a problem that's going to go away soon. The irony is that we can't read data that we wrote half a decade ago, but 500-year-old books are just as legible today as when Mr. Gutenberg first moved the type for them.

The best advice is if you really want to preserve something forever, write it down.

Ants

I have always admired ants. I love the way they organize themselves into teams to get the job done. I love the way they leave an invisible scent trail behind so they can follow each other in a straight line. I love the way they communicate with each other by touching antennae. I love the way they can lift a billion times their weight. And I love the way they send out little scouts to find food, returning with a report of some new tasty treat that the queen will love.

In my house, however, I absolutely detest ants with every fiber of my being. They are disgusting little scavengers. They can't be killed fast enough. They overtake the tiniest crumb left on the floor and then they scamper all over the kitchen without even a polite "Please, sir, can I have some more?"

I live on the very edge of suburbia. My back yard opens up to a lake-front development, whose homeowner association demands money of me every year, offering me a swimming pool in return, which I have yet to ever visit. My front yard opens to a hay field and other assorted agriculture beyond. Being on the frontier of civilization means that I occasionally have to tangle with miscellaneous vermin attempting to invade my domain.

None of them are as hideous as the ants.

My front porch is especially susceptible to their advances. Ants don't eat good wood, but they sure love the taste of decaying carbon life forms. Through an unfortunate mixture of building code violations and generally bad engineering, I have needed to replace several boards on my front porch as they rot away. And each time I discover a new board that has "bit the dust" under a million layers of paint, I have discovered a nest of ants that have decided to take up a tasty residence inside. Evil, nasty creatures they are.

And somewhere — I still haven't found it — there is a crack between my deck and my dining room. Every once in a while, a scout ant finds his way through that crack and starts snooping around in my kitchen. If he finds the smallest morsel available to him, it's only a matter of hours before he has summoned a million of his brothers to form a conga line and enjoy the feast.

This isn't intended to be a commercial, but I'll swear, there is one and only one product that does any good. Forget the traps, forget the sprays, forget the bait. If you have ants like I do, get a tiny bottle of Terro Ant Killer. You have to get the bottle; the traps by the same name are worthless.

You get a three-ounce bottle of a thick, clear liquid, about the consistency of molasses. Put a drop of that stuff on a small piece of cardboard or paper and place it directly in the path of the ants. As soon as they discover it, the magic occurs. Their first reaction is, "Wow, this is really good stuff!" Kinda like the first time you discovered Krispy Kream donuts. They stand there and suck it up like pigs eating Twinkies. Man, it's a sight to behold.

Their next reaction is to race home and tell all their brothers. Of course, in the process, they take home a present to their mom. And bang! Overnight the whole colony looks like the day after a frat party with no hope of recovery. A sweet sight to behold.

I keep a bottle of that stuff in my kitchen. If I see even one stray ant, I whip out the bottle and I make sure he "discovers" the meal I have created for him. I can't afford to let them get out of control. No tolerance. One ant equals a drop of Terro.

Remember that name: "Terro Ant Killer". They didn't pay me for this endorsement, but maybe they should.

Who Chooses Your Music?

In the beginning, all music was religious. After all, there was no other reason for music to exist except to please God — or the gods, in the case of the ancient Greeks. If you wanted music, you went to church. You kinda had to like what music they had there because that's all there was.

The *church* chose your music.

The Renaissance came and went and we were all thusly enlightened. So royalty took over the music industry. Music came out of the churches and went to the castle. If you were a peasant, you may hear something coming over the walls around the moat. But for the most part, musicians were hired by nobility and were thusly at their service.

The *king* chose your music.

It pretty much stayed that way for a long time. The masses had some folk music. But the really good stuff was for the wealthy. It wasn't until the first part of the 20th century that recorded music became available, which finally gave music to the masses. In fact, it wasn't just *available*, it was downright ubiquitous. The Muzak Corporation decided that people worked better when they listened to boring music. Thus, they had the honor of seeing their corporate trademark devolve into a generic term for bland, retail music — heard everywhere, including elevators.

Corporations chose your music.

When rock and roll came around, radio stations learned that they could win the hearts of teenagers by playing their music. Soon, dozens of music formats filled the airwaves. You still couldn't pick your songs, but at least you could pick your genre. It was now possible to retreat to your car during lunch and tune into whatever you wanted — at least, you could if they were playing it.

Radio stations chose your music.

Now you can put your entire music into a little box the size of a pack of cards. Two skinny wires can connect your ears to literally thousands of songs for your listening pleasure. You can control what songs to listen to, in what order, and how loud to listen to them. Heck, you can even choose to "shuffle" them (play them randomly) so it sounds like you're actually listening to radio. But it's *your* radio, the way *you* like it.

You chose your own music.

When people plug into MP3 players, it is often because they want to withdraw from society. They want to create their own little reality inside their heads. Music gives them an opportunity to do that.

It's ironic that in olden days, the church and the nobility isolated the populous from music. Now that it's available for mass consumption, people use music to isolate themselves from the rest of the world. The isolated has become the isolator. Have we really made any progress?

Just for Feet

A few days ago, I worked in the yard for a couple of hours. The grass was damp and my tennis shoes were, uh, a little porous.

I came inside to do some more work. After a while I realized that I wasn't comfortable, but I couldn't figure out why. I walked around thinking to myself, something is wrong. What is it?

Finally, it dawned on me. I went upstairs, took off my soggy socks, and put on a pair of clean, dry, white socks. Ahhh, much better.

Pay attention the next time you watch the news and they interview somebody who has been kidnapped, or lost in the woods, or drifting at sea for a long time. What's the first thing that they usually want — after they get a hamburger from McDonald's?

They want a pair of clean, dry socks.

It's been said that the eyes are the window to the soul. Acupuncturists tell us that the feet are the path to your internal organs and thus, all happiness.

An old saying goes: "Ain't nobody happy until Mama's happy." A natural extension to that is: "Mama ain't happy until Mama's feet are happy."

It's true. Offer any woman a foot massage. None of them will refuse it.

Have you ever noticed that some people are "shoes" people and some people are "not-shoes" people? I know some people that declare that the first thing they put on in the morning and the last thing they take off at night are their house slippers. They are never without something on their feet. I know other people that declare that the first thing that comes off their feet when they get home are their shoes. They're the ones that sneak from their cubicle to the printer and back wearing socks.

Both groups are equally adamant. Their feet control the way they organize their lives.

What is it about feet that make them such effective determinants of our happiness?

I think it's because they are the foundation on which we literally stand. The health of a house can be measured by its foundation. And the health of a person is often determined by the health of their feet. It's easy to forget about them — they're just so darned functional. So I think every once in a while they remind us exactly how important they are.

Sometimes — just to get your attention — the feet have to say, "Hey, these socks are a little damp. Hey, hey! A little attention please! We're choking down here."

See? The only tool they have to communicate is by signaling discomfort. It's a special language that they've developed to get attention. And it's very effective.

Answering "That" Question

Any parent who has a young child full of questions spends a great deal of time waiting for "that" question.

The exact definition of what "that" question is varies from one parent to another. It really doesn't matter. You know what I mean. You're not really sure if you want your child to ask "that" question. You think you've rehearsed a pretty good answer. But what if it's not right? What if there's a follow-up question? What if the answer isn't satisfactory? What if it's taken the wrong way?

The best a parent can do is to rehearse the answer over and over again until it becomes second nature. Don't panic. Don't draw too much attention to the question. Answer it casually. Answer it coolly. Perhaps a one-off sentence will suffice. This time. Maybe you'll get lucky. Who knows?

But you've got to be ready.

We were driving home tonight when my nine-year-old son — completely out of the blue — said, "Dad, I want to ask you *a very important question*."

Uh, oh. This is it. He's going to ask "that" question. Okay. Get ready for this. What did I promise myself I'd do? Oh, yeah. Don't over-react. Casual. But make sure I appear to be genuinely concerned. After all, it was important enough for him to ask. I have to demonstrate that I'm actually paying attention. But not too much.

I turned off the radio. That's my universal signal to him that even though I have to keep my eyes on the road, he has my undivided attention.

"Okay, son, what's your 'important' question?" Here it comes. Grip the steering wheel. Eyes straight ahead. Don't over-react.

"Which would you rather eat: poison ivy? or a mosquito?

"Uh, a mosquito, I guess. It'd be a lot smaller. In fact, it'd probably be so small you'd hardly even notice it."

"Yeah, that's what I thought, too. Besides, I wouldn't want to get poison ivy all down my throat because I wouldn't be able to scratch down there."

"That's a good point."

"But sometimes mosquitoes carry diseases."

"Well, sometimes they do, but not very often. The chances that the mosquito that you would eat would be carrying a disease would be pretty small."

"That's true. Mom said that she'd rather eat a mosquito, too."

"That's nice." Whew, at least I agreed with his mother. That was a relief.

Okay, it wasn't *"that"* question. I'm still waiting for that one. But I guess I cleared up the whole mosquito/poison ivy problem that had been vexing him for some time.

On the way home, we bought some ice cream. I doubt that he ever really understood why.

This Information Highway is Super

I am constantly amazed at the power of the Internet. I had an experience today that reminded me of some of my very first Internet experiences.

In the mid-1990s, I was just starting to figure out what all the Internet stuff was all about. I had been programming mainframe computers for years. We had always noted with a certain amount of pride that computers were like "islands". They had a vast amount of processing power within them. And, oh yeah, if you wanted to move data between them, that's what tape drives were for.

But now I had my brand new Packard-Bell computer, complete with Windows 3.1 and a 2400 baud dial-up modem. A friend of mine had shown me a really cool program called "Netscape". I was ready to impress people.

Of course, the easiest person for me to impress was my mother. So I hauled her into my office. I was going to show her this Information Superhighway that Al Gore was talking about.

I only knew about one site, a search engine called "WebCrawler". Look, Mom. All you have to do is type a topic into this screen and it will go out to the Information Superhighway and find out everything there is to know about it.

I will never forget what happened next. Of all the things that I could have demonstrated to my mother, for some weird reason I picked — are you ready? — "Meg Ryan". Look, Mom. Let's see if there's anything at all out there about "Meg Ryan".

I pressed "enter" and 3.276 seconds later, a list of Meg Ryan pages came on the screen. Dozens and dozens and dozens of pages. I thought she might be mentioned in one or two places. But there they were. There were Meg Ryan pictures. Meg Ryan movies. Meg Ryan scripts. Meg Ryan fan clubs. There was a whole universe of Meg Ryan in my office in front of my eyes and Mom's eyes.

I don't know who was more surprised, me or Mom. No, it was me. Mom responded with a polite "That's nice, dear." My eyes were huge and my chin was on the floor. Oh, my God. What has just been invented, and I didn't even know about it?

That was my first OMG experience with the Internet.

In the intervening years, there have been several others. But for the most part, I have come to expect that literally the world of information is at your fingertips if you have an Internet connection.

Just think of the places to have your questions answered. You want a real expert to answer? Go to www.allexperts.com, pick an expert, type in your question, and you'll have a response in a couple of days.

Can't wait? Type your question into answers.yahoo.com. It's like yelling a question into a room crowded with people. Within minutes, half a dozen people will have responded.

Want to clarify the meaning or spelling of a word? Mr. Webster is waiting for you at www.m-w.com.

Want to read a more seminal article about just about any subject from aardvarks to zymology? Check out www.wikipedia.org. My son has done research for complete homework assignments without ever leaving the Wikipedia site.

Which brings us to my current astonishment. A few days ago, a friend of mine told me a joke. I wanted to re-tell it, but I wasn't sure exactly how it went. Could I possibly find something as mundane as an insider musicians' joke on the Internet, knowing only the punch line?

Yep. I typed a couple of words of the punch line into my favorite search engine (I'm a Yahoo! guy — Google is for snobbish wimps. Real men search with Yahoo!), and there it was. Not only the joke, but four or five variations of it. The same joke in slightly different settings, slightly different set-ups, but the same punch line.

I shouldn't be amazed. I should come to expect it. But I do this stuff for a living and I still don't understand how it all works.

The Internet gives us jokes, facts, pornography, civics, movie critiques, MP3 files (free and pirated), weather reports, sports scores, driving directions, and advice for the forgotten and the forlorn. All mixed together like noodles and tomatoes in goulash.

I think my generation has done a pretty good job of gathering and delivering all this stuff. It's up to the next generation to sort it all out.

Unpopular Presidents Just Can't Win

Few presidents are popular while they're in office. Even less so in their second term.

Even John Kennedy, who barely won an election over Richard "I-am-not-a-crook" Nixon, didn't enjoy overwhelming popularity when he was in office. History was kind to him because he was martyred. If he'd had a chance for a second term, he would have been totally ineffective.

His successor, Lyndon Johnson, realized that and got out while the getting was good.

George Bush is currently experiencing that phenomenon. His popularity numbers are in the toilet and he still has a couple more years of lame-duckness ahead of him.

When interpreting popularity numbers, it helps to remember that there are really three types of voters in America. There is the left, the right, and the middle. And they are approximately evenly divided. About a third of us are basically liberal, about a third are basically conservative, and the rest are somewhere in the middle.

Which brings us to the fallacy of popularity polls in presidential politics. When a politician says they don't pay much attention to the polls, that usually means they are lying. But at the same time, a politician that is really true to his principals shouldn't worry about polls for two good reasons. First, it's a game he can't win. And second, his job should be to serve his constituents, not to be "popular".

The biggest problem with polls of this type is that they ask a question that is usually interpreted differently by either side of the political spectrum. The basic question is usually something like this:

> "Do you generally *approve* or *disapprove* of the job that (politician "X") is doing?"

No matter what kind of job he is "doing", those on the opposite side of the spectrum are always going to answer "disapprove". After all, that's the whole idea of politics, isn't it? To make the other guy look like an idiot? No matter how well a politician is performing, he usually won't score much more than 70% because a third of the people are going to hate him no matter what. In school, that's usually about a C-minus.

But here's the dirty little secret. Many people on the *same* side are also going answer "disapprove". Why? Because the guy isn't *enough*. He's not liberal enough or he's not conservative enough. Kinda hard to win that way, huh?

Some of Bill Clinton's harshest critics while he was in office was from the far left, who thought he had sold out his principles to the Republican-led Congress, especially on issues such as Welfare reform and NAFTA.

And many critics of Bush are from the far right, saying that he has sold out his constituency on issues such as limited government and border security.

Remember those thoughts the next time you look at Bush's — or any president's — numbers hovering below 50%. Many times, that's not a sign of a president not doing a good job. It's just one that is meandering too much in the middle while pleasing nobody on the fringes.

Why Doesn't Water Burn?

Every first year chemistry student knows that water is composed of two parts hydrogen and one part oxygen. That's what that "H-two-oh" thing is all about.

In our chemistry classes, we also learned that hydrogen is just about the most combustible thing out there. You know the story of the Hindenburg and "Oh the humanity" and all that.

And we also learned that three things are needed to create a fire: fuel, oxygen, and heat.

And any third grader knows that you can put out a fire by pouring water over it.

Waitaminnit. Am I the only one to see a paradox here? You put out a fire by pouring two-thirds of the formula for fire on it? Gee, it seems like water should be a tinderbox, just waiting for a match to turn it into a lighter-than air blazing inferno.

What gives? Well, if you just sorta mixed up the hydrogen and oxygen then, yeah, you'd have a ball of gas that's ready to light up like a Kuwait oil field. But that's not what water is. The hydrogen and oxygen form together at the *molecular* level.

In a union that is only fully understood by God, atoms can bond together to form something completely different — something that didn't exist before. Something that that has absolutely no characteristics of the original raw materials.

God allows us to use electrolysis to break the hydrogen and oxygen apart. But He bonds them together so tightly that it usually requires more energy to break them up than what is yielded in fuel. When God sticks things together, He generally doesn't mess around.

In the book of Second Corinthians, the Apostle Paul tells us that "if any man be in Christ, he is a new creature". The implication is that we are made into a new species, literally something that never existed before, something that has no characteristics of the original raw material.

I guess God knows what He's doing. After all, He can take the most perfect fuel in the universe and turn it into a pretty good fire extinguisher.

Children Don't Have Governors

When I was a teenager, I mowed lawns for a living. Like most teenage boys, I had an obsession to take apart internal combustion engines any time I was around them. I didn't know anything about what I was doing, but sometimes my Briggs and Stratton mower found itself in pieces in my back yard, just so I could figure out how to put it together again. Luckily for it (and for my career as a mower), I always managed to get it back in working shape without too many parts left over.

One of my discoveries was a nifty device that I later discovered was the engine's governor. It was a spring loaded paddle attached to the throttle and located next to the cooling fan. As the engine turned, the fan blew air against the paddle and the throttle opened and closed appropriately.

If the engine speed slowed down, the fan blew less air, and the spring on the paddle moved it closer to the fan. This opened the throttle a little bit, giving more gas to the engine, which increased the air and moved the paddle back to its original position.

If the engine sped up a little bit, the paddle moved the other direction and the throttle delivered less fuel. You get the idea.

This delicate balancing act kept the engine at a somewhat constant speed. When mowing tall grass, the engine would slow down slightly, but the governor would deliver a little more fuel, preventing the engine from stalling. The governor also kept the engine speed in check by guaranteeing that no more fuel was being delivered than what could safely be burned.

It doesn't take much technology to impress me. I'm always having those gee-why-didn't-I-think-of-that experiences. I was struck by the fact that the governor didn't actually measure the rotation of the engine. Rather, it measures the *effect* of the rotation — the wind that was created. And the wind was actually just a by-product of the natural cooling of the engine by the fan. I was amazed at the simplicity and the economy of the unit.

As an adult, I discovered that children don't have a governor. It's not something that's "built-in" to a kid when they are born. It's something that comes from experience. It's a sign of maturity.

Children don't know how to "measure" their own activity. They live for the moment, indifferent to the consequences. I had a teacher in college that put it this way: Children only know two words — "Me" and "Now".

The next time you're at an amusement park, notice how many parents are carrying sleeping children on their shoulders at the end of the day. How can they possible sleep with all this excitement around them?

Lacking any built-in controlling mechanism, children spend all their energy as soon as there is an outlet for it. They ride every ride. They eat every hot dog. They gobble every cotton candy. They have no idea how tired they are or how sick they are becoming. They cannot measure it for themselves.

Finally, equilibrium kicks in and the body shuts down. Asleep on Dad's shoulder, they ride home in the back seat, dreaming of the fun they've had.

The same thing happens with teenagers and video games. As they are consumed in the moment of the game, they have no idea of the effect it is having on them. They play and play and play until their brains are mush and their thumbs are as brittle as toothpicks.

It is our job as adults to be the governor for children. It would be nice if each of them had an energy meter in their forehead. Or a zombie meter in the case of teenagers. Or something that would let us measure the effect the activity is having on them.

But no such meters exist. Instead, we can measure them only indirectly. The lawn mower governor didn't measure the engine, it measured the effects of cooling the engine on the atmosphere and made adjustments accordingly. In the same way, we need to search for clues in our children's behavior and the effect they are having on the environment around them so we can let them know — in the most loving but parental way — that enough is enough.

Death by Rotting

In America, we are a land of rules and laws. Most of the time, those laws make sense. Sometimes they have unintended consequences. And sometimes things don't seem to work out the way we think they should. But it's the best system that's available and we're gonna stick with it.

We're a land where juries often have the final say. That goes all the way back to the Magna Carta, which gave the accused the right to be tried by his peers. The prevailing wisdom is that a group of well-informed, impartial citizens usually make the best decisions. Most of the time, it works fine, even though every once in a while it means O. J. Simpson gets to play golf unfettered.

Juries often make decisions regarding punishment of criminals. Judges may occasionally soften the punishment, but they can never make it harsher. One particular case was recently in the national spotlight and deserves some commentary.

By all accounts, Zacarias Moussaoui is a creepy guy. He was arrested just prior to the 9/11 attacks as a possible terrorist while he was a student at a flight school. It seems that his flight instructor had notified the FBI after being suspicious of Moussaoui's competence and motivation. No kidding. He was probably a lot more interested in learning how to navigate than to actually take-off or land the plane.

We'll probably never know exactly what his involvement in the plot was supposed to be. At one time, he denied all involvement. Then he said that he was supposed to fly a plane into the Capitol. For a while, he was somehow related to Richard Reid's shoe.

At least we know he didn't like America. You're not supposed to yell "Fire!" in a crowded theater. And screaming "You will never get my blood. God curse you all!" in a crowded courtroom full of people that are deciding your fate usually isn't a good idea, either.

So the jury was supposed to figure out whether we should give the guy a potassium chloride cocktail or if we should just let him rot in a jail cell for the rest of his life.

They decided on rotting.

The whole death penalty argument is one that has fascinated me through the years. After all, it is appointed to all men to die. So we really can't invoke a death penalty; we can only cause death to happen sooner than it would have naturally. And on our own terms.

Some will argue that we shouldn't spend money keeping prisoners alive that have no possibility of ever seeing civilization again. But it can't be a strictly economic decision because the conviction and appeals process probably costs more than a bed and three square meals every day for the next forty years or so.

Some people actually have a death wish, so executing them is a favor to them. You can kill two birds with one stone — so to speak. The criminal gets his wish and society gets its revenge.

In Moussaoui's case, it seemed to be a matter of relevance and knowledge. The more he knew about the planned attacks — the greater his involvement — the more he deserved the ultimate penalty: death.

But the jury decided he really didn't know that much. He knew enough to get life in prison but — irrespective of what he claimed in his own "defense" — he didn't know enough to deserve to die.

Pundits immediately spun that by saying that a life of solitary confinement was actually a sentence worse than death — which is exactly the opposite of what the jury intended.

Either way, Zach had determined that he was going to win. If he was executed, he would die a martyr and get his 40 virgins. If his life was spared, he could claim to have gotten away with it against the evil empire. And hey, that's probably worth at least a dozen or so virgins.

He felt that he had a right to be defiant at his sentencing hearing when he declared, "America, you lost. I won."

But Judge Leonie Brinkema had the last word. She said that everyone else in the room would be "free to go any place they want. They can go outside and they can feel the sun, smell the fresh air, hear the birds. They can eat what they want tonight. They can associate with whom they want. But you will never again get a chance to speak and that's an appropriate and fair ending. You will die with a whimper and never get a chance to speak again."

The House Always Wins

It's been said that gambling is cheap entertainment for people who are poor in math.

It doesn't take much sense to know that, in the long run, the house always wins. Always. They wouldn't play if they didn't. They're smarter than that. Many times, the same can't be said of their customers.

It's true that in the short run, it is possible to make more money in a few seconds than what the CEO of Exxon makes in a year of retirement. The chances of that happening are almost negligible. Let's just assume that's not going to happen in your lifetime. Or mine.

Which brings us to today's story from the Associated Press. In 1991, John Daly entered the PGA Championship as the ninth alternate. That's kinda equivalent to starting the Indianapolis 500 on the outside of the 33rd row. Or starting a Major League Baseball season with the word "Royals" on the front of your jersey.

In other words, he wasn't expect to win. But he won. Instant success. Instant fame. Fans everywhere. Endorsement contracts. Okay, so he wasn't a Tiger, but he had a pretty comfortable life.

In the next 15 years, he won a total of five PGA Tour victories. And he lost somewhere between $50 and $60 million dollars gambling. I can't even imaging earning that much money, let alone losing it.

He's rehabbing now, but he's gotta be looking over his shoulder saying "Wow, I coulda been rich!"

Daly tells the story of last fall when he won $750,000 in a tournament, drove to Las Vegas, and promptly lost $1.65 million in five hours. How does one do that, you ask? By playing $5,000 slot machines. He was actually betting more on one pull of a handle than most cars that I have bought. And he was doing it over and over and over.

He tells another story about how he lost $600,000 in 30 minutes. What was his response? He borrowed another 600 grand from the casino. It took him two hours to lose that.

At one time, Daly owed $4 million dollars to casinos. Fortunately, he won the 1995 British Open. The earnings from that paid the casino debt. I guess the tournaments were kinda like an enabler, letting him make stupid decisions and then bailing him out of them.

During the time he was doing all this gambling, he was still playing a winning golf game. But his earnings from golf totaled "only" $8.7 million. I guess wearing all those Nike shirts made him enough money to play his stupid little games.

Okay, I'm not going to get into the moral aspect of gambling. But if you decide to treat it as "cheap" entertainment, at least practice "safe" gambling. Set yourself a "walk-off" limit and stick to it.

Approach the floor with only a certain amount of cash in your pocket and expect to lose it all, because you will. Play that money, have fun, get your free drinks.

And when that money is gone, get up, thank (and tip) the dealer, and get out of there as fast as you can.

Enjoy your memories of the eye candy and adrenalin rush.

Next time, do the math and ask yourself if it's really worth it. If you think you can afford to lose $60 million on earnings of $8.7 million, go for it. The Associate Press will do an article about you. And I'll have material for another blog entry.

Julie is not Lisa

Just when you think you know a song, you run into it years later and, bam! you realize you had it all wrong.

Well, maybe not you. But it happens to *me* all the time. After all, this forum is about what I think.

Back in 1975, Jessi Colter (better known as the wife of Waylon Jennings) had a melancholy country/pop cross-over hit, “I’m Not Lisa”. I’ve always liked that song, and I used to think I knew what it was about.

I recently heard it on the radio again, looked up the lyrics on the Internet, and had one of those “hey, waitaminnit” experiences.

All I remembered about the song was the classic opening lines: “I’m not Lisa, my name is Julie.” I was so lazy, I just stopped listening there. I put the song in the genre of “guy-calls-new-girl-by-old-girl’s-name-and-barely-lives-to-regret-it”. Been there. Done that. It’s not a pretty sight.

But that’s all wrong. It’s a beautiful love song. Not a song of jealously or envy. Or even forgiveness.

It’s a song of *unconditionally love.* Of understanding. Of empathy.

And that’s the best kind.

Here it is:

==============================

I’m Not Lisa
by Jessi Colter

I'm not Lisa, My name is Julie.
Lisa left you years ago.
My eyes are not blue, but mine won't leave you
Til the sunlight has touched your face.

She was your morning light; her smile told of no night.
Your love for her grew with each rising sun.
And then one winter day, his hand led her away.
She left you here, drowning in your tears,
Here, where you stayed for years crying Lisa, Lisa...

I'm not Lisa, my name is Julie.
Lisa left you years ago.
My eyes are not blue, but mine won't leave you.
Til the sunlight shines thru your face.

==============================

The song is saying this:

"I know I'm not your first love. You were madly in love with her. And that's okay. But she's gone. She left you. Somebody stole her heart from you. That hurt. Bad. I know it did. I can't do anything about that.

"But you know what? I'm never going to leave you. I'm never going to hurt you the way she did. I'm going to stay with you forever. No, I'm not your first love. She was. But I'm here now. Love me."

Man, wouldn't everybody love to have a "Julie". Somebody who will smile, love, and say it's going to be okay. Forever.

Upside Down with my Son

When my son was a toddler, he thought the world revolved around him, which is SOP for kids of that age. So when he wasn't getting enough attention, he would do whatever it took to draw attention to himself. This caused some problems when I needed to stay late after church to talk to anybody. With my son in tow, I would try to conduct my business with other church members. And he would, well, he would want to toddle.

Parents do what they have to do to get their kids to obey. You just kinda sorta gotta do whatever it takes. That's why parenting classes aren't always effective. Every child is different and every relationship with their parents is different.

In our case, I discovered that he could be distracted if I carried him upside down. I don't know what it was, but whenever he was being fussy and I couldn't devote as much attention to him as he thought he deserved, I could get him to obey by picking him up and simply turning him over. Something about the blood rushing to his head, or the sudden attention that he was getting, or maybe just the change in perspective would satisfy him and I could continue my business.

So that's what we did. I talked to people at church carrying my son upside down. It became almost automatic. It was so easy to reach down and turn him over; I could do it without even thinking and without breaking my conversation.

Soon I came to be known in our church as the guy who carries his son upside down. I guess everybody's got to be known for *something*.

Eventually, it extended to our nighttime routine. He would come downstairs in his pajamas and announce that he was ready to go to bed. That meant that I was supposed to carry him up the stairs to his bedroom — upside down.

Over the years, he grew up and I carried him less and less — upside and otherwise. My back and my knees appreciate that fact, but I kinda missed it.

He's nine years old now. A couple of nights ago, he said he was ready for bed. I asked him if he wanted me to carry him upstairs to bed. I saw that he hesitated a little bit. "I won't carry you upside down. Just regular." Okay, that was probably okay. "I'll let you if you want to."

If I want to?

What had started out as a disciplinary procedure had turned into a cherished ritual. And now it was in danger of extinction. My little boy was growing up and he was losing one more aspect of his child-ness.

But he was wiling to revert to being a toddler for just a few moments — if it made his dad happy.

I carried him upstairs, my knee aching the entire time. My back finally forgave me when we got to the top of the stairs and I laid him in his bed.

That's probably the last time I'll carry him up the stairs. I guess we'll have to find something else to build some more memories.

Tipping

The most insane of all Western customs that exists today is that stupid little practice known as "tipping". Whoever first came up with this asinine idea should be paid minimum wage and then should be tied up and have unimaginable things happen to him as everybody passes by, bribing him for better service by waving dollar bills in his face.

Depending on the circumstance, the idea of tipping is either:

a) to bribe a service provider to give you with superior service

or

b) to reward a service provider for providing such service.

At least, that's what they'd have you believe.

Okay, so why do I have to tip the doorman at a hotel for carrying my bags? Isn't that his job? If I don't tip him, what's he gonna do? Drop them down the elevator shaft? Maybe the idea of the tip is so he provides service genteelly. Is that what I'm doing? Paying a buck a bag for a smile?

And why am I supposed to tip the skycap if he takes my bag at the curb, but not the ticket agent if he takes my bag at the gate? And what about the poor guy who's actually in the hot sun or blizzard-like cold throwing my bag on that conveyor belt that leads to the belly of the plane? He probably works harder than all of us, but he doesn't deserve a tip because he doesn't get a chance to smile at me? That's ridiculous.

Since I have a hard time figuring out tipping of bell staff and baggage handlers, I've taken to always giving them their tip as wadded up dollar bills. They always smile and cram their reward in their pocket, feigning humility as they salute me with a tip their hat. Hopefully, my dollar bill will get mixed up with everybody else's and they won't know if I tipped them one dollar a bag or five dollars a bag or twenty-five cents a bag.

See? The tipping system is so out of whack that I have resorted to crumpling George. I should be ashamed.

I never have to tip the front desk people at a hotel. They smile without it. They're polite. Heck, they usually even speak English intelligibly, unlike any taxi driver I have ever met. But they don't need a tip. They just do their job. Duh. Like they're supposed to.

What about casino dealers? I win a big hand so they think they deserve part of it? Like they had something to do with my luck? Did they put their money at risk? No, they just happened to be there.

But the silliest of all is waiters and waitresses. I know, they're in a strictly service job. You're totally at their mercy. Or they're totally at your mercy. Or something like that. But they're *supposed* to provide good service. They're *supposed* to smile. It's part of their job. Why should they have to be bribed to do it?

The room service menu on a hotel I recently stayed at says that a 20% gratuity is added to every bill. 16.57% of that goes to the delivery person and the remainder goes to the kitchen and support staff. Where in the world they came up with that formula, I have no idea. But that doesn't stop them from having their hand out when they deliver my meal, begging for more. It's insane.

Why can't the restaurant owners just pay the wait staff what they're worth? Makes sense to me. What? That would increase the price of the meal? Would that put anybody out of business? The price of a $5.00 hamburger would go up to $6.00. Would anybody notice? Probably not. But I'd be so happy at the prospect of not having to figure out a tip that I might just eat there every day.

So here's the punch line. Workers: Do your job. I don't get tips for my job; why should you? Employers: Pay people what they're worth; let the economics level the playing field for all.

It just makes sense.

New Car Smell

I got my car washed today. Notice that I didn't say I "washed" my car. I can't remember the last time I "washed" my car.

I take it to one of those full-service car washes. At this one, you pull up and talk to a well-groomed college kid — five years from now, he's going to be a vice president at some bank or maybe a top salesman in his district. You decline the special that they're having today on detailing and hand-waxing, take a receipt from him, and turn over your car for the bath of a lifetime. It goes into a long tunnel where it is showered, scrubbed, polished, and rinsed.

It emerges from the other side, drenched but generally happy. Then about three or four more college boys pounce on it to give it a good rubdown. (In ten years, they will all be CPAs working for Mr. Order-Taker on the other end of the tunnel. But today, hey, working at a car wash pays better than spending your summer as a life guard.)

When they are done, they signal that your car is ready. You press a few dollar bills in their hand — nobody knows why, but everybody has to do it. And then they ask you "the question".

"What fragrance would you like today, sir?"

The answer, of course, is always the same.

"New car."

If people would stop and consider what the "new car smell" really is, they probably wouldn't be so excited about it. It's actually a complex combination of volatile organic compounds including several varieties of glue, solvents, and paint. Mix that with some fumes from freshly-curing leather and vinyl, bake it with sunlight in an enclosed environment for several hours each day, and you have a delightful aroma — sure to please your senses and remind you of the first time you sat in the car and look down, noticing an odometer that registered fewer than ten miles. What a treat!

There's a good reason why we treat the new car smell with the same sense of denial that forbids us from thinking about what's really in a hot dog. The reason is because the sense of smell is one of the most effective triggers for memories — usually fond memories. The source or the toxicity of the smell are overcome by the association to the memory.

And the association with "freshness" is one of life's greatest joys.

A friend of mine once told our department secretary that she smelled like a freshly-mopped floor. It was intended as a compliment and she took it as such. She knew that "freshness" was the true association with the smell. It didn't matter if she smelled like Ajax or Mr. Clean or Glade. The fact was that she smelled "fresh", and that's all that mattered.

Anybody over the age of 40 remembers the fresh aroma of a page printed by a spirit duplicator. Sparkling white paper and fuzzy blue ink were the rule of the day when I was in school. It didn't matter that your algebra test was printed with a 50/50 combination of isopropanol and methanol. The fact was, you knew everything was going to be okay because, well, the test smelled “fresh”.

People are making millions of dollars today because they have perfected car odorants that smell like volatile organic compounds and women’s perfume that smells like Lysol.

I think I could make a bundle if I could invent a spray that smelled like a ditto machine. Image the sniffing that would happen in my next meeting if I were to spray the agendas before I passed them out. We’d probably have to adjourn the meeting early, just so everybody could go back to their cubicles and inhale to their heart’s content in blissful privacy.

The Uh-Oh Second

In this world of micro-seconds, nano-seconds, and pico-seconds, it is becoming more and more important to measure increasingly smaller units of time.

I've heard that the smallest measurable unit of time is the time between when the light turns green and the guy behind you begins to honk.

I have determined that there is an even smaller, more definitive unit of time. I call it the "Uh-oh second".

An uh-oh second is the unit of time between when answer "Yes" to the computer's question "Are you sure" and you realize you weren't. Uh-oh.

You just deleted a file that you didn't intend to. You just exited a program. You just closed a session. You just completed an order. Your credit card just got billed. Whatever. You did it. It's too late.

The uh-oh second can be applied to many other aspects of life. It's the time between when you slam your car door shut and you realize your keys are in the seat. It's the time between when find yourself pouring catsup on a hot dog and you realize that your son had asked for mustard.

It's the time between when you complete drilling a 3/4 inch hole and you realize you should have drilled a 3/8 inch hole. It's the time between when you introduce your new wife to your best friend and you realize you just used your ex-wife's name.

Uh-oh.

I discovered a whole new genre of uh-oh seconds recently when I purchased a new shredder for my home office.

The office trash can is a wonderful invention. It's a kinda purgatory for paper. It's the place where paper goes when you don't think you need it any more, but before you're really ready to give it the official heave-ho to the landfill.

But privacy concerns — and a burning desire to experiment with a new source of mulch — lead me to replace my office trash can with a brand new Fellowes shredder. This is the one that they advertise on television with a bulldog confetti-making machine, making a mess of the office to the delight of the owner. "Good boy."

What I learned very quickly about office shredders is that they are very unforgiving. Instant judgment.

Credit card solicitation. Rrrrip. Another credit card solicitation. Rrrrip. Home equity loan solicitation. Rrrrip. Mutual fund solicitation. Rrrrip. Credit card bill. Rrrrip.

Uh-oh.

The shortest measurable unit of time is the time between when you shred a bill that you need to pay and you realize you have no idea what in the heck that was that you just shredded, but it must have been something important.

Purgatory never looked so good.

Systematically Learning About "Systemic"

A few months ago, I had a problem with bugs in my bushes. So I made a trip to my friendly lawn and garden store and explained my problem. An associate at the store reached up and pulled off a bottle off the shelf. "You need a systemic pesticide. This will take care of it for you."

I consider myself to be somewhat of a master of the English language. I try to use words like "ubiquitous" and "esoteric" in everyday conversation just to keep people around me on their toes. But I absolutely hate admitting in public that I have no idea what's going on. So there was no way that I was going to admit that I didn't know what "systemic" meant.

Assuming the store clerk knew more than I did, I bought the potion, sprayed it on my plants, and the bugs curled up and melted away. Oh well, who needs linguistics when chemistry works?

Some time after that, I heard some people talking at work about their bug problems at home. "What you need is a systemic pesticide", I overheard. Hmmm... Well, I still don't know what it means, but it must have something to do with killing bugs. So that's good enough for me. I filed it away in my brain with the definition of other horticultural things and went on with my life.

A few days ago, I was listening to some political commentary on the radio. The analyst said that corruption in Congress was "systemic".

Waitaminnit. What does pesticide have to do with Congress? Obviously, there is more to this word than I originally thought. This demands some investigation.

I discovered that "systemic" comes from the original Greek word that means "to combine" and is related to other English words such as "system" and "synergy". They all have something to do with the bringing together of disparate things so that they act together. Makes sense.

In agriculture, a "systemic" pesticide is one that is absorbed into the sap of a plant or the bloodstream of an animal which is harmless to the host but which renders it toxic to invaders. As an extension, it can be applied to anything that is rampant throughout an organization to the degree that it affects the body in general — such as the usage when applied to corruption in Congress.

The Tower of Babel aside, human language is essentially an invention of, well, humans. As such, it is an imperfect creation, but one that is rich in history, tradition, and culture. English as we speak it today has only been around for a few hundred years. Deciphering the language of our Founding Fathers only 250 years ago can be somewhat of a challenge.

But that's part of the charm of the language. There is a wonderful serendipity that results when we discover that the same word can be used in reference to pests in the garden as well as to pests in politics. And we can trace it all back to ancient Greece.

I hope I never learn everything there is to know about English. It would be a shame to think that I already know it all and that there are no more mysteries waiting to be unraveled.

Rocking with Ringo

Men deal with mid-life crises in many different ways. Some men have an affair. Some buy a new convertible. Some quit their job and go on a world-wide cruise.

I brought a drum set.

I've been a musician my entire life. I think I've played the piano ever since I could read. And I've been a percussionist for the last 15 years or so.

But I've always wanted to be a *drummer*. My best friend in high school was a drummer. I had hung around drummers all my life. But I remained safely ensconced in the confines of timpani, congas, tambourines, and xylophones. All the while, I yearned for the free-wheeling and controlled-frantic feeling that only a rock drummer can enjoy.

So, being of sound mind, proper financial means, and appropriate motivation, I brought a drum set, a few sticks and cymbals, and yes, a copy of "Drums for Dummies" — just to keep from totally embarrassing myself.

How does one practice drums without a band or a regular venue in which to perform? I bought a set of sound-isolating headphones with an extra-long cable. I plugged it into my stereo, tuned the radio to the local "oldies" station, and started rocking to the greatest hits of the 60s and 70s.

With a little practice, I got pretty good. Soon I was playing along with the Beatles, the Stones, Elton John, Linda Ronstadt; it really didn't matter who or what was playing. If it came on the radio, I rocked along with it. There was something comforting — fulfilling — about finally living the dream of being a great rock musician, even if it was only in my own mind.

One night, I was playing along with the Beatles' "Let it Be". Suddenly, I was struck with a sense of awe that took me quite by surprise.

I was playing drums with Ringo Starr.

It was almost like Ringo was right in the room with me, smiling approvingly as he watched his protégé learn his trade, albeit late in life. I literally had to stop for a moment and, with my hands to my side, listen to the symphonic orchestration of Ringo's percussion for the rest of the song.

Ringo had already established himself as a great drummer before he was with the Beatles. John and Paul actively sought him out to be in their band. They knew he was exactly what they needed to round out their little group of musicians. And with the addition of Ringo, the Fab Four from Liverpool spent the next seven years rewriting the history of rock music.

In his early days, he played with a four-piece kit rather than the standard five-piece — eschewing the middle tom-tom. Even though he is left-handed, he played with a right-hand setup, often leading with his left hand. These innovations gave Ringo's style a distinctive sound as he influenced the development of early rock-and-roll drum music.

Ringo understood that the role of a drummer in a rock band is a supportive one. His playing was never in the forefront, was never ostentatious. But if you listen closely, you'll hear him doing things in the background that are so creative and so unique that it is no wonder he remains one of the most influential rock drummers even today.

And that's exactly what I do. As I'm playing along with the radio, I'll play just about any song that happens to come along.

But when a Beatles song comes on, it's more likely that I'll just be listening. Listening for inspiration. Listening to learn.

Thank you, Ringo, for everything you've taught me.

Mayor Bloomberg and His Money

Michael Bloomberg is the mayor of New York City. And he must have really wanted the job, because five years ago he spent $74 million on his campaign to get it. His own money.

He must have liked the job once he got it, because last year he spent $85 million to get reelected. His own money. That comes to about $113 per vote.

Mr. Bloomberg founded one of the largest and most successful financial information companies in the world and has a personal wealth of more than five billion dollars. So he can afford to drop a few million here and there on extraneous ventures. He doesn't need to work another day in his life. So he has decided to lead the largest city in the world's last remaining super power. The city that sits in the middle of a red bulls-eye for every terrorist organization with a plane ticket or a stick of dynamite.

When studying elected leaders, we are often urged to "follow the money". The prevailing wisdom says that politicians are usually beholden to the whims of those who put him in power. That makes sense when the major contributors are labor unions or fringe activist groups.

But what does it mean when the major contributor is the politician himself? It can't be that he needs the job to support his ego; there are much easier (and cheaper) ways to have one's ego stroked. It's not just a power grab. In spite of his great potential power, he still regularly rides the subway to work. And it certainly isn't because he needs the money. Refusing the traditional mayor's salary, he receives a token one dollar per year in compensation.

Bloomberg seems to be one of those rare breeds who actually is a public servant because he feels like he needs to *serve the public*. He spent his own money to avoid the repressive campaign finance reform laws that limited his opponents. As a result, he doesn't owe anybody anything. Nobody can buy him. Nobody can influence him. He can stand on his own principles and govern in a way that is most beneficial to the people who elected him.

New Yorkers must like him. The staunchly liberal city reelected this Republican by a 20% margin last year.

You gotta admire a guy that puts up 17% of his entire personal worth to get a thankless job in a city that should be suspicious of a rich corporate suit. My hat's off to him.

The Original Diet Coke

In 1963, the marketing guys at Coca-Cola had an interesting problem. Coke needed to respond to the Royal Crown Cola Company, who had come up with a fairly successful product known as Diet-Rite Cola. Today we take diet versions of cola for granted. But in the early 1960s, that was a revolutionary concept. All these bikini-clad girls were suddenly concerned about their figure, but they still wanted to drink their favorite beverage without guilt. Substituting cyclamate for sugar seemed like a good plan.

So the product development department at Coke got busy and developed what was essentially Coca-Cola without the sugar. All that was left was to put it in a bottle, stick it on the grocer's shelves, and kick some Diet-Rite butt with a 300-pound gorilla marketing plan.

Waitaminnit, said the Suits. What are they going to call this stuff? They can't just call it (gasp) "Diet Coke". After all, they had spent millions of dollars protecting and preserving the honored, hallowed, cherished Coca-Cola brand. To dilute it by putting the word "diet" in front of it would be — well, it would be heresy! (Today, we would call it "brand extension" — think "Honey Nut Cheerios" — but that was a foreign concept at the time.)

So they turned to the market research department. Come up with a brand new name for this product. Some short, snappy, memorable. And do it quick! We can't afford to have Diet-Rite eat one more fraction of a percent of our market share.

(Meanwhile, the execs at Pepsi were watching all this with a combination of amusement and blissful ignorance. It would be a couple of years before "Diet Pepsi" showed up on the market — with no apparent concern about diluting a trademarked name that had been playing second fiddle to Coke for years.)

The marketers at Coca-Cola huddled in their conference rooms in Atlanta, shuttering and shivering at the thought that they might make a marketing blunder. This was too important of a job for mere mortals. They must call upon the gods. The gods of IBM.

At the time, the IBM 1401 was a relatively new workhorse. It was the size of an average living room and had been introduced as a "business" computer, as opposed to a scientific computer. It was used to maintain customer records at banks and actuary tables at insurance companies. It was a 6-bit machine that contained a maximum 16Kb of data in its core memory. (For perspective, a typical two-page Word document is about 20Kb in size. Yes, folks, this computer could just about hold this entire article in memory.)

The folks in the IT department were eager to find creative uses for their new toy. So they were overjoyed when the marketing department asked for their help. Could they use their brand new computer to generate a list of all possible four-letter word combinations?

The geeks put their slide rulers to work and their pencils to paper. Did they realize that would generate a list of 456,976 words to chose from? Back to the marketers. Hmmmm... Okay how about a list of four-letter words that contain only one vowel? Back to the slide rulers. Okay, that would be a list of only 192,000 words.

So the computer went to work. Disks whirred, tapes spun, lights dimmed. Green-bar paper spewed from high-speed printers. Long hours, late into the night.

Finally, the list was delivered. Marketing poured all over it, eliminating unpronounceable and potentially offensive words. Brows sweated. Pizza was consumed. Tensions rose.

Finally, they emerged with the winner. The new product was going to be named...

"TABB!"

The creative guys got their hands on it. Okay, that could work because they could use the double-entendre of keeping "tabs" on the calories that are consumed. But the extra "B" was kinda in the way. A logo was invented with distinctive capitalization: "TaB". Yeah, that's it. Genius!

The rest, as they say, is history.

The geeks were left scratching their heads. Hey, we thought they wanted a *four*-letter word. If they had asked for a list of *three*-letter words — gee, that would have generated only (putting the slide-ruler to work again) 17,576 potential words to pick from. Why can't anybody in the marketing department get their requirements established before they ask us to do all that work?

The IBM 1401 computer is now legendary with computer history buffs. Today, you probably have more computing power in your wristwatch than the machine that named Tab. In fact, doing the research for this article, I wrote a macro in Excel that duplicated the effort. It took me about three minutes to write and 3.5 seconds for my computer to execute.

But this represented one of the first successful joint ventures between a marketing department and a computer department and is thus worthy of historical note.

Of course, 40 years later, IT still doesn't do what marketing initially asks for. And marketing still can't write user requirements that they can live with through the end of the project.

Some things never change.

Buying Cred

Many years ago as a high school student, I gave piano lessons to my little brother for a few weeks. It was a big mistake. I'm surprised that we still talk to each other after all these years.

When it came time for my son to take piano lessons, I wisely opted myself out of candidates to be his teacher. There was no way that I was going to put my fatherhood on the line by trying to assume the role of piano teacher.

And the reason why? In my son's eyes, I lacked credibility, or "cred" as it's known on the street. (With the bro's in the 'hood, why should one use five syllables when one will do?)

The funny thing about cred is that you first have to *earn* it. Then, after it's earned, it must be *purchased* to be effective.

Consider this. If you have some problem — personal, financial, professional, whatever — the last person you should go to for advice is a close friend or family member. You need to go to someone who has *earned* cred. That's probably somebody with a degree, with appropriate experience or training, or somebody that is recognized as an expert in his field.

Even if you're fortunate to have an expert in your family who has earned cred, they probably aren't a good candidate to help you because of the other requirement — you have to *buy* the cred from them. It doesn't do any good to get advice from somebody unless you have some "skin" in the game. And the way you get "skin" is to pay for it.

Countries with socialized health care systems are learning this the hard way. When you have to pay for your medical advice, you tend to ration your need for it. The system balances itself naturally.

But when health care is free, the patient has nothing at risk. Even though the doctor has *earned* his cred by going to medical school, the patient isn't required to *buy* his cred. With nothing to lose, there is nothing stopping the patient from consuming the product (in this case, health care advice) with aimless abandon. Soon the health care system is overloaded and would collapse if not for some sort of mandatory rationing.

Ask any doctor in Canada and they will tell you that their day is filled seeing perfectly healthy people that just want to have somebody to talk to. And nothing is stopping them from doing it because they have nothing to lose. They aren't required to buy the "cred" from the doctor, so the system is imploding.

Back to the piano lessons. I may have earned my cred with my brother and my son, but neither of them had to buy it from me. So I was irrelevant and ineffective.

"Son, I think you should practice each hand separately on that song and then put them together only after you have mastered each one."

"No, Dad. That's not the right way to practice piano."

See? No cred.

A couple of months later...

"Son, I'm glad to see that you are practicing your hands separately now."

"Yeah, that's the way my piano teacher told me to practice. It works so much better than trying to learn them both at the same time. I'll put them together after I have learned them separate from each other."

Same advice, different results. His piano teacher has cred. His dad — me — well, my cred might as well be crud for all it's worth.

Dixie Hockey

I woke up this morning to the news that the Stanley Cup finals for the National Hockey League ended last night. And the winner was Carolina.

My first thought — after I realized they were still playing hockey in the middle of June — was, *Carolina has a hockey team?* Isn't the land of Raleigh/Durham/Cary/Chapel Hill the domain of Duke and North Carolina and NC State? Do they even know what a puck is? Heck, do they even know what *ice* is? Do they know how to play any sports down there that doesn't include a 10-inch round orange ball or a football-shaped brown, uh, *foot*ball?

And for Pete's sake, they beat some Canadians. Not wimpy French "Canadi*e*ns", as they're known in Montreal. These are real manly Canadians: the Houston, er, I mean Edmonton Oilers.

Shoot, the Canadians practically *invented* hockey. They actually understand the definition of "icing". And they know how in the heck somebody can be "offsides" when there are men skating all over the place instead of starting each play lined up neatly on each side of the ball, uh, puck. I think the Canadians deserve to win just for being cerebral enough to understand the game.

But wait, there's more. It turns out this wasn't just a Dixie-vs-Cannuck fluke. Yessir, ladies and gentlemen. Last year's Stanley Cup was won by ... (are you ready for this?) ... the Tampa Bay Lightning. That's right, they actually play hockey in Florida!

Sheesh, next you'll be telling me that they play baseball in Montreal. Waitaminnit. That's right. They actually *used* to play baseball there, but nobody noticed. So they moved the team to Washington DC.

God bless America. At least Major League Baseball finally figured out what sport belongs where.

Now, if we can only convince the NFL to restore the St. Louis Cardinals, the Los Angeles Rams, and the Baltimore Colts to their rightful locations.

The Golden Rule of Business

Most of the work that I do is project-related. A project is identified, a team is assembled, and a team leader is chosen. Some projects last only a few days; some go on for months. They all overlap so I'm usually working on several projects at a time in various stages of completion.

One project team I was involved with had one very uncooperative team member. Although he claimed to be working on the project's behalf, it was very obvious to me and to the other team members that he was much more interested in drawing attention to himself. I was the one on the team that had to work the closest with him — which meant that I had to put up with most of his foolishness and cover for many of his mistakes.

The project leader knew of my problems and was sympathetic to them. But in the best interests of getting the work done, we all agreed to do the best we could with what we had to work with — even if that meant putting up with the rudeness and incompetence of the most uncooperative team member I have ever worked with.

Toward the end of the project, the team leader caught me in a particularly "down" mood, pulled me aside, and said "Joe, it's nice to have somebody like you on my team."

What a breath of fresh air! With one statement, I learned what the project manager was actually looking for. And received a "stroke" to make me feel better.

As the project progressed, I watched the other team members' behavior, compared it to my own, and put myself in the position of the project lead. I soon realized that the best behavior would be one that I would want if I were the leader of the team.

Obviously, "Mr. Uncooperative" didn't understand that concept. I can't believe that he would actually want himself on his team. Certainly, he wouldn't want a whole team of people like himself. Nothing would ever get done because everybody would be fighting for attention for themselves.

When you were young, you probably learned something about the Golden Rule: "Do unto others as you would have them do unto you." With this project, I realized that the rule works in business as well as it does in personal relationships.

I learned that the best way to be a team member is to be the type of member that you would want to have on a team. I now measure my behavior on a team with the question, "Is that the type of behavior that I would want a member of my team to exhibit?" All I have to do is remove myself from the process, turn around and look at myself, and observe what I am doing.

If the Golden Rule of life is "Do unto others as you would have them do unto you", the ancillary Golden Rule of Business should be "Be the type of team member that you would like to have on your team."

Why No Pope Joe

I have always been proud of my given name. There were several great men named Joe in the Bible. Joe was Jesus' earthly father. A guy named Joe donated the tomb in which they laid Jesus to rest. And that fellow in the Old Testament with the Technicolor Dreamcoat was named Joe.

So when we got a new pope last year, I was excited that his name was Joseph Ratzinger. There had never been a Pope Joe before. At last, this fine name had a chance to be recognized in all its papal greatness.

But waitaminnit. Cardinal Ratzinger decided he didn't like "Joe". He was going to go down in history as Pope Benedict XVI. There would be no Pope Joe I.

Needless to say, I was crushed. "Benedict" may be a fine name in Vatican circles, but in American culture, it conjures up images of the traitor, Mr. Arnold. Nobody names their kid "Benedict" any more. Benjamin, perhaps. But Benedict sounds so 18th century.

That got me to thinking about why popes are named the way they are. Why don't they like the names their own mother gave them? And what's with all the X's and V's and I's? So I did a little research.

It can all be traced to a 6th century monk named Mercurius. He had the distinct misfortune of being named by his mother after the Roman god Mercury. Poor kid. He might as well have been named Darth Vader. All the other kids in seminary laughed at him.

That is, until they he was elected pope. Funny how life-changing events like that turns everybody's perspective around.

Knowing that he was due the last laugh, he could have gone on with his life as Pope Mercury. But there was something, well, sacrilegious about that. It was a legacy that he couldn't bear to take credit for.

So he started a new trend. He decided that he should be named after his favorite ex-pope, who had reigned just a decade or so before. Nobody was going to argue because, hey, he's the Pope. And that's how Monk Mercury became known as Pope John II.

The Catholic Church treats tradition with as much respect as Tevye's prayer shawl. So when one pope decides to do something, most of the others follow suit. For that reason, virtually every pope after that has assumed the name of some previous pope. There's really no reason for it. It's just something that Mercury, I mean, John II did. And it seems like a quaint little tradition to uphold for 1500 years.

But all those Roman numerals get messy sometimes. After all, there's a finite number of names to pick from, so they start getting reused rather quickly. And it seems like every other one likes the name John. Or Paul. Or John Paul. Which brings us to an interesting story about Pope John XX.

When popes first started borrowing names from each other, nobody cared much to keep track of everything. (The marketing geniuses at the NFL figured out that numbering Super Bowls with Roman numerals was pretty cool; the marketing guys at the Vatican weren't that on the ball.) After a while, there were a bunch of Johns and Pauls and Stephens piling up and somebody decided to make sense of it all. So here come the Roman numerals.

But that got even more complicated with anti-popes and the Holy Roman Empire (which was neither Holy, nor Roman, nor an Empire). How do you count the guys that laid claim to the papacy but that were later found to be heretics? Or how do you count heretics that were martyred although they were later found to be true men of God?

It took several hundred years to sort it all out. After a bunch of arguing about who's "in" and who's "out" as a pope, they settled on a bunch of numbers to give everybody.

And all was fine until the year 1276 when Pedro Hispano — the first Portuguese pope — wanted to be called John. Oops. They found out that he was only the nineteenth Pope to be named John, but there was already a Pope John XIX. So for some reason, they decided to skip a number and Pedro became John XXI. For that reason, there is no Pope John XX. And there never will be, either.

There'll probably never be a Pope Joe I, either. I think that's a shame. It's such a nice name.

How Knives Work

Have you ever wondered how a knife works? How is it that a machine as simple as a blade of metal is able to accomplish things so elegantly that we could only do with brute force?

Take, for example, a steak knife. If you want to eat a steak, you have the option of picking it up in your fingers and ripping off bite-size pieces to put in your mouth. But isn't it much more neat and convenient to have a knife neatly slice through the meat, giving it a clean edge and a perfectly sized piece? How does it do that?

Everybody knows that a knife is better when it's "sharp". What does "sharp" mean? It means that the edge comes to a definite point instead being rounded.

Consider it this way. When you push down on a knife, you exert force through the knife onto the piece of meat. Let's say that's a force of, oh, five pounds or so. But it's not just five pounds. That force is spread over the surface area of the meat where the knife meets it.

Hang in there. We're getting close to understanding how this works.

Suppose you lay the knife on its side and push down. That five pounds of force is now spread over the surface of the knife blade — perhaps two or three square inches. Not much cutting power there, huh? Just a mushed-up piece of meat.

Now turn the knife on its sharp edge. Push down with the same force. That same five pounds of force is still being exerted on the meat. But instead of being spread over two or three square inches, the force is concentrated. Let's see — how much area do you think is represented by the *edge* of the knife as opposed to the *side?* Infinitesimal, don't you think? And the sharper the knife is, the less surface area is represented by the edge and the more concentrated the force is.

Knives work not because they are strong, but because they concentrate all their strength in a very small area.

There's a lesson to be learned from this. When we are in a struggle, it often isn't important how strong we are — individually or collectively. What really makes us effective is when all our strength is concentrated in a small area. The greater the concentration, the more effective our relative strength.

"Sharpening" our skills doesn't refer to making us stronger, smarter, or better. It means learning how to effectively utilize the skills that we already have — concentrating them in a small area — to get the job done.

Katrina was not a Hurricane

A few days ago, I heard the voice of a commentator on the radio railing about global warming. Giving examples of receding glaciers and rising sea levels, he said "Katrina was just the beginning!"

A few days later, I saw a similar article in the paper. "If you thought Katrina was bad, just wait till you see this year's crop of hurricanes spawned by the fastest rise in global temperatures in centuries."

As bad of a storm as it was, the fact that these commentators are forgetting is that the tragedy of Katrina was not that it was a hurricane.

Most of the people that died in Katrina actually died a couple of days after the storm struck. They were the people that foolishly stayed behind and drown in the flood.

Most of the property damage was not the result of buildings being blown over. The buildings were destroyed by the resulting flood that left them standing in water up to their eaves for weeks after the storm went by.

Did you catch that? Katrina was not a *hurricane*. It was a *flood*.

Hurricane Katrina hit New Orleans as a Category 3 hurricane, somewhat weaker than the Category 5 Hurricane Andrew that barreled across Florida over a decade ago. It was an unfortunate coincidence that a slightly stronger-than-average hurricane hit a heavily populated area. A little more to the east or west and it would have been a lot different story. A slightly stronger or weaker hurricane would have created a completely different scenario.

But there it was. A monster, but not the biggest monster ever. And not the product of increased global temperatures. Just an average hurricane that wandered into the wrong area of demographics. Literally a meteorological bull in a china closet. The bull doesn't know how he got there or what damage he was doing. He just wants out. And that's what Katrina was. She didn't aim for a large population area; it just happened to be in the way.

The real tragedy was the failure of the levees.

Thousands of people had weathered the storm in their homes. Thousands more had sought refuge in the Superdome. And they all lived through the storm, wandering outside the next day to a clear sky and an uncertain future.

But then the levees broke. There is plenty of blame to pass around for the failure of the levees. They were managed by corrupt, disjunct local authorities who failed to communicate with each other. The Army Corps of Engineers now has evidence that they weren't as structurally sound as they originally thought. The city of New Orleans failed to spend money properly that had been allocated for their maintenance. The federal government failed to properly oversee the distribution of that money. Everybody failed to heed years of warnings by engineers and in the local press that the entire levee system was a disaster waiting to happen.

Add to that, the population of New Orleans had suffered through years of corrupt Democratic rule which had trained them that the government was the solution to all their problems. So when they were told to get out of town, a large number of them decided to sit and wait, thinking they were going to be cared for. When the local government collapsed and the federal government was slow to respond, they had nowhere to turn, because they had no means or inclination to help themselves.

Katrina was a massive failure of engineering, government, and society which exacted a toll of epic proportions on the property and the population of New Orleans. But please, don't use the words "Katrina" and "global warming" in the same sentence. They have nothing to do with each other.

Message to AARP: I Don't Need You

This year, I celebrated one of those dreaded birthdays with a "zero" in it. Turning over a new decade is kinda like walking down a hallway in an office building and then rounding a corner. Everything is familiar, but suddenly different at the same time.

What do I get for my half-century of life on this planet? I am deluged with offers to join that most dreaded of all liberal organizations, the AARP.

They don't like to be called their former name, the "American Association of Retired Persons". They discovered a few years ago that they could get more members if they target "old" people, rather than "retired" people. Of course, they define "old" as anybody over 50. (We younger old people tend to hang around longer — less attrition, you know.)

So the AARP (Don't you just love that acronym?) wants me to join, eh? Well, they can save their money. I have long known that AARP (It just flows from the tongue, doesn't it?) is an ultra-liberal organization, much more interested in selling their services to finance their left-wing causes than they are in actually providing value to their membership.

In their marketing literature, the AARP (Aaaaaarp! They should fire the marketing department that came up with that name!) lists 22 specific "benefits" that I would receive by joining. I won't bore you with all 22. Here are the highlights; the most comical benefits from AARP (Sounds like a cat with a fur ball, doesn't it?) and the reasons why such benefits are totally irrelevant in my life.

A subscription to the bi-monthly magazine, *AARP The Magazine*. This thing used to be called *Modern Maturity*. They took a magazine that sounded like it belonged in a nursing home and changed the name to a combination throat-clearing sound and a redundant noun. I think I'll write a book and name it the "Auugggghh Book". It would make as much sense.

A subscription to the *AARP Bulletin* to "keep informed on current legislation and issues that affect you most." Like cradle-to-grave government health care and other failed socialist programs.

Access to the AARP web site. What, is there something there that I can't get anywhere else on the Internet for free? Have they never heard of WebMD? Or Google?

Savings on hotels, motels, resorts, airfares, cruises... The list goes on. A combination of Expedia and PriceLine is all I need.

Know that AARP is standing up for your rights like fighting predatory home loan lending. Oh, they're protecting stupid people from making stupid investments.

Low-interest credit card. I haven't paid a dime of interest to a credit card company in years. When you come out with a NO-interest card, I may be interested.

AARP endorsed auto and homeowners insurance. Just because an insurance company paid

AARP to endorse them doesn't make them a better deal.

Pharmacy services with convenient delivery to your mailbox. I haven't taken a prescription drug in ten years. When I do, Walgreen's is just down the street.

Rewarding volunteer opportunities. What? I need to *pay* to join an organization to *volunteer?*

AARP safe-driving course. Now they're insulting my perfect driving record!

Reduced cost health insurance. They actually think it'd be a good idea for me to buy health insurance from a company whose primary customers are old people who consume 85% of all health care expenses in this country. That makes about as much sense as buying dental insurance from the NHL Player's Association.

Sorry, AARP. You have nothing for me. You can save a bunch of money by not marketing to me.

Try me again in another 25 or 30 years, when I'm *really* old. I won't listen to you then, either. But I could probably use another good laugh by then.

What Makes a Joke Funny

I have always wanted to write and get something published. There have been times that I thought the best way to do that would be to submit something to Readers' Digest. After all, every issue practically screams the words "Earn $300! Just send us your funny stories."

Some of the stuff they publish is pretty lame. It's real easy to take the "gee-I-can-do-better-than-that" attitude. And they've made it so easy now with online submissions. Just go to their web site, fill out a form and click on "submit". You don't even need a stamp.

So a few weeks ago, I submit what I think is just about the funniest little ditty I know. It goes like this:

Roses are red,
Violets are blue.
Most poems rhyme
But this one doesn't.

I thought it'd be a perfect addition to RD's "Laughter, the Best Medicine". Or maybe it could be one of those little snippets they put at the bottom of the page when they can't quite stretch an article to fit.

Apparently, the folks at Pleasantville don't share my enthusiasm for humor. I never heard a word from them. Oh, well. Their loss.

At least the experience caused me to think about what makes a joke funny. And it gave me an excuse to write about it.

I have been told that to be funny, a joke has to have a sense of exaggerated reality. That's what makes the comic strip "Family Circus" so funny. Everybody can relate to Bill and Thel as they try to raise their four young children in a house with two dogs and a cat. Haven't we all pointed to a panel that we thought was particularly funny just because it was *so dang true?*

That may be one quality of humor, but I heard Bob Hope give another explanation that was equally true. He said that good humor often rests in its timing. The longer you wait before revealing the punch line, the funnier the joke will be.

He gave this example. In the late 1950s, the Cold War with Russia was at full steam. The Russians were sending satellites into space with alarming frequency. Meanwhile NASA was alternately blowing up rockets on the launch pad or ditching wayward spacecraft in the ocean without ever achieving orbit.

In one of his shows, Hope decided to poke honest fun at our misfortunes. Here's the entire joke:

"Hey, have you heard the latest good news coming out of Cape Canaveral? They just successfully launched a new submarine!"

(Insert rim-shot here.)

The joke is rather dated now, but at the time it was hilarious. In a fraction of a second, the audience was on the edge of their seat only to be duped.

Good news from Cape Canaveral? Hey, we could sure use some good news right about now. Those nasty Ruskies are hammering us in the space race. Who knows what kind of nuclear stuff is floating around above our heads right now? Yes, Bob. Please tell us. What is this great news of which you speak?

They just launched... Great! They launched! They finally got one of those Roman candles in the air! Oh, I feel so much better now. And they launched a ... a *what?*

Oh, a submarine.

Heh, heh. Very funny.

By successfully delaying the punch line until the *very last word* of the joke, Hope successfully turned a national embarrassment into good-natured laughter, teaching me a lesson in humorous timing in the process.

Now, look back my submission to Reader's Digest. "But this one doesn't." I think that's a great punch line. Delayed as long as possible. Definitely funny. Definitely worthy of inclusion in any fine literature.

Oh, well. I'm not going to quit my day job, waiting for somebody to realize my creative genius.

The Marketing of Redeployment

A friend of mine who had served in the military told me that there are three ways to do everything: the "right" way, the "wrong" way, and the "military" way.

The fact is that the military has a different way of doing several things. And they can get away with it because, hey, they're carrying weapons and I'm not.

For example, the military has words that mean things only to them. In the military, you don't eat "food", you eat "rations". They aren't served in a "cafeteria", it's in a "mess hall". And when you're done eating, you don't "clean" the area, you "police" it.

The military doesn't "move" troops, it "redeploys" them.

Enter the Democrats.

Nothing would please the Left more than if we would pack our bags and leave Iraq right now. Or at least say that we're going to leave next July 1st. Or April 1st. Or something. The point is they want to get out of there.

But Democrats develop foreign policy based on focus groups. And the focus groups don't like the word "retreat". They also don't like "surrender". They don't like "defeat". And they sure as heck don't like "cut-and-run". Sounds too "girly", you know.

Notice that it doesn't matter what word the Democrats like. It's what the *focus groups* like that matters. They learned their lesson from the Republicans during the Vietnam conflict when Nixon tried to convince everybody that "Détente" was a good thing. Most people simply shrugged their shoulders at that French word, leaving Nixon and Kissinger wondering why they hadn't listened to the focus groups and called their strategy "can't-we-all-just-get-along?".

Back to the present. The Democrats needed a term that they could use that would mean, "Oops, we're outta here. Good luck with your new constitution, y'all!" without sounding chicken.

Somebody at the DNC opened a military manual and discovered the word "redeploy". Hey, that works. We're not retreating; we're just "redeploying" our troops. We're just moving them to a place where they can be more effective. Yeah, that's it.

In their fight for public opinion, they have taken a word that has a very specific technical meaning to the military and have marketed it as legitimate foreign policy. And they're doing a great job with it.

Somebody should tie a Democrat to a chair and read the Constitution to him. Although Congress can declare war and authorize the spending thereof, nowhere is the authority to direct troop movement given to them. That still belongs to the "Commander in Chief". That's why he's called the Commander.

The framers of the Constitution feared a government controlled by the military, so they wisely put the military under the control of civilians. But they also realized that a camel is a horse that was designed by a committee. You can't have 435 elected representatives telling the military what to do and when to do it. For that, you need a boss.

You don't have to agree with everything that President Bush has done in the execution of the war. But leaving Iraq prematurely would create a vacuum that would throw the country into anarchical chaos. And announcing a withdrawal timetable would simply signal to the insurgency that they have extra time to accumulate weapons, recruit teenage boys, and throw some of those charming IED-building parties that they're famous for.

No, we owe the people of Iraq better than that.

Empty Space

Space is really big. And it's really, really, really empty.

If you look at a detailed map of our solar system, you'd think that it's pretty crowded between the orbits of Mars and Jupiter. There are thousands — millions — of little planetoids and asteroids floating around out there. Some of them have wonderful, exotic names like "Massalia", "Alexandra", "Petrina", and "Seppina". Others have sterile, provisional names like "(29075) 1950 DA", "(3360) 1981 VA", and "(15760) 1992 QB1". It seems as though the sky should be filled with them.

As we started sending spaceships to Jupiter and beyond, many people expressed dismay that our daring little robots would be pelted to smithereens by flying space rock. As a child, I remember seeing movies where spaceships would fly through asteroid belts and it was like pushing your way through the crowd in the mall on the day after Christmas to buy wrapping paper at half price.

But after 30-some years of trans-Jovian exploration, not one craft has been as much as brushed by a pebble. Have we really been that lucky?

No, space is really *that empty!*

Cosmic scales are really hard to imagine. Let's put it in perspective.

If the sun were the size of a basketball, the earth would be smaller than the round head of a push-pin. And it would be about 100 feet away.

And what would be between the two? Nothing. Well, Venus and Mercury would be floating around — even smaller than the earth. But they'd be just as likely as not to be floating around on the other side of the sun — far, far away. The largest of the asteroids would be smaller than dust particles in smoke.

Space is so empty that the odds of a spaceship being struck by a stray asteroid are literally billions to one against. You have to try really hard to catch up with an asteroid. We've sent a couple of craft specifically to track some asteroids. And we've gotten some good pictures of them as a result. But it ain't easy, even when you're trying.

So the guys at NASA had a special challenge recently with their New Horizons spacecraft. It was launched last January and is currently speeding toward Pluto faster than any craft has ever traveled before. So fast, in fact, that it's already going through the asteroid belt.

The New Horizons project team wanted to have a chance to test some of their navigation and imaging equipment. After all, there's not much else to do while you're coasting along on the way to the most distant planet in the solar system. So they decided, hey, if we're going through the asteroid belt, let's see if we can spot one.

Yep. They weren't concerned about *being hit* by one. They were trying to even *find* one.

Quite by coincidence, they found a tiny asteroid that they were flew close enough to track. They found and photographed asteroid 2002 JF56. It's a little rock, about one-and-a-half miles across. At the time, it was more than 63,000 miles away. The most powerful of New Horizon's digital cameras resolved the asteroid only to a couple of pixels.

So a casual cruise through the most densely populated neighborhood of our solar system yielded a chance encounter with a tiny rock tens of thousands of miles away. The paradox of space is that it is both crowded and empty at the same time.

Delegation and Control

I always have fun when I get to perform in musical or drama presentations for church, school, and civic groups. And I can usually learn something as I watch how the leaders of the production manage the process of "herding cats".

There are probably no two groups in the world that have bigger egos than thespians and musicians. (Well, maybe politicians, but that that's a whole nuther subject.) When you get thirty of them on a stage, you'll have at least fifty different opinions on how a scene should be performed.

The secret to good management is knowing when to *delegate* and when to *control.* I saw that perfectly illustrated in a recent rehearsal.

One scene was going particularly poorly and was restarted several times as new problems arose. Finally, all progress came to a halt as the assistant director, choreographer, music director, and several cast members argued about how to proceed.

The director of the play had been watching from the rear for some time without offering much help. After all, he had successfully delegated the responsibility for this scene to several of his underlings. And opening night was only a couple of days away. Finally, however, he realized the situation had reached an impasse.

He ran to the stage from the back of the room. "Hold it, everybody. This is *my* decision!" Then he waved his arms in a controlled frenzy. "You go over there. You stay there. You enter from there. Now. Let's try this again from the top of the number!"

Then he turned around, walked to the back of the room, and took his place on the back row to watch the rest of the rehearsal.

Everything went smoothly from that point forward. The director didn't *seize* control. He *restored* control. He knew that he had placed the right people in areas of authority. He gave them all the rope they needed. But he also realized when enough was enough. He exercised just barely enough control to nudge the project back into sanity.

And he provided me with a perfect example of the appropriate way to manage my business, my family, and my life.

Frogs, Drowning, and Risky Behavior

Here is one of my favorite jokes — one that demonstrates how one can be presented with the facts in a logical manner and still reach the absolute wrong conclusion.

A young science student decided to experiment on a live frog. He placed the frog on an observation table and said, "Jump, frog! Jump!" The frog jumped eight feet.

Then the student cut off one of the frog's legs and said, "Jump, frog! Jump!" This time, the frog jumped six feet.

He cut off another leg and said, "Jump, frog! Jump!" The frog jumped three feet. He cut off one more leg and said, "Jump, frog! Jump!" This time, the one-legged frog could hop only a few inches.

Finally the student cut off the last of the frog's legs and said, "Jump, frog! Jump!" The frog did nothing; he just stared blankly at the student. "Jump, frog! Jump!" Once again, nothing. The frog didn't move.

So the student wrote in his notebook: "When all the legs of a frog are cut off, the frog becomes deaf."

Another example of possibly coming to the wrong conclusion involves the recent news item. It reported that 80% of all drowning victims are male. If you're not careful, it may be tempting to conclude that women are better swimmers than men.

But I believe it has more to do with the way a man's mind is wired than anything else. Men are inherent risk-takers. Given a set of possible actions, a typical woman will generally choose a safer alternative than a typical man. Women want stability and security; men want challenge and excitement.

So men are more likely to drown simply because they are more likely to put themselves in a position where drowning is a possibility. It has nothing to with their physical abilities and everything to do with the choices they make.

Since risk and reward are so highly correlated, that explains why men seem to be at the polar extremes of almost every category. It explains why men dominate boardrooms and lists of the wealthiest people. It also explains why prisons and homeless shelters are filled almost exclusively with men. Men choose risky behavior and are more likely to accept the rewards and suffer the consequences for their actions.

See? If you stick around me, you'll be sure that you'll always come to the correct conclusion.

Cats

I have had the pleasure this month of performing in a local community theatre production of "Cats", Andrew Lloyd Webber's record-breaking Broadway musical.

Cats has been rightly criticized for its apparent lack of plot. But I'll cut it some slack. After all, it is a collection of T.S. Eliot's poetry set to music with great choreography and a stunning wardrobe.

But what it lacks in plot, it makes up for in its study of human behavior — vicariously through the minds of felines.

The musical concerns itself with the tribe of cats known as the "Jellicles" as they prepare for their annual gathering at the "Jellicle Ball". Every cat in the tribe is introduced individually as the audience slowly becomes aware of the distinct behaviors and personalities of each.

I have been especially drawn to the three oldest cats of the tribe — and I have been intrigued by the treatment each of these cats gets from the younger ones.

Old Deuteronomy is the oldest and wisest of all the cats. He's the patriarch of the clan; heck, he's probably the father or grandfather of many of the kittens. He is held in the highest esteem, virtually worshiped by all as he makes his appearance.

Gus is a "theatre cat". He's like the old uncle that shows up at the family reunion with old war stories — except that Gus' stories deals with all the great theatrical parts he's has played through the years. The kittens adore Gus and clamor around his feet, purring over his every word.

And then there's Grizabella, "The Glamour Cat". She has led a hard, hard life. Her coat is dirty and mangy, she walks with a weak shuffle, and her eyes are sunken and sallow.

None of the cats like Grizabella. They shun her. They ignore her. They gnash and snarl at her. The old cats pull the kittens away from her and the kittens shirk back in fear. It's a sad, sad, sight.

I always wondered why the cats treated Old Deuteronomy and Gus with such high regard, but they were always downright mean to Grizabella. The director of our local production finally gave me the answer.

Grizabella made all the wrong life choices. She left the tribe many years ago, seeking her own fame and fortune. She once had a life of glamour and charm and beauty. But she gave that up, seeking something more. In the process, she turned herself into a shell of what she used to be. She spent her fortune, she wasted her life, she prostituted her body. In the process of seeking more, she lost everything she owned.

Now she has returned to the tribe, seeking kinship. But the cats will have none of that. They have spent their lives acting like respectable cats. They have played by the rules, they have led a good life, they deserve to be called whatever they want to be — and Old Deuteronomy reminds us in one song that the proper term is simply ... "Cat".

The cats love Old Deuteronomy and Gus for what they *are*. But they hate Grizabella for what she *did*. Perhaps they show no mercy, but you can hardly accuse them of being bigots. They realize that cats are ultimately responsible for their own actions. And the lesson to be learned is that there are always consequences for one's actions — even if those consequences are harsh by our human standards.

In the end, Old Deuteronomy, in his supreme wisdom, redeems Grizabella and allows her to enter the "Heaviside Layer" — a place of reincarnation for the most-worthy of all cats. In doing so, he teaches the tribe a profound lesson. Whereas they hated Grizabella for *what* she did, he loves her *in spite of* she did.

That is a lesson we should all learn.

Microsoft Brands

A fundamental lesson you learn in Marketing 101 is that it is rarely a good idea to brand a product with a generic name. In other words, you can't just put some tap water in a pretty bottle, invent a snazzy logo and brand it as "Water".

Marketers often invent completely new words like "Kodak" or "iPod" for their product. If they feel like they need a generic word, they usually misspell it slightly to give it a distinctive feel. Like "ReNu" or "Embarq" or "Chex".

But if your title is "The Richest Man in the World" (seriously, that's what's on his business card), you don't have to follow conventional wisdom.

So when Microsoft created their new graphical operating system based on a series of windows that allowed multi-tasking, they named their product, uh, "Windows". Real catchy, huh?

Seizing the opportunity to establish new standards of chutzpah in name branding, they created a pretty cool word processor and named it "Word".

They didn't stop there. Their graphics program is called "Paint". Their project management software is "Project". Want a calculator? They've got one. It's called "Calculator". If you want to explore the Internet, you'll need a program called "Explorer". Want to edit a photo? Try "Photo Editor". And if you have some media that you want to play, the best choice is a little ditty they call "Media Player".

If you have an office in which you want to run most of these software programs, you'll find they've been neatly combined into a nifty little package named “Office”.

About the only time they actually came up with anything original is when they developed presentation software. For some reason that I’ve never understood, it’s called “PowerPoint”. I guess you use it to make a powerful point. I dunno.

I’ve decided that I’m going to compete against Microsoft on their own turf. I’m going to write the world’s greatest graphics-based word processor. It will be three times better than “Word” — much more granular. I’m going to name it “Syllable”. Or maybe “Alphabet”.

My lawyer told me that I needed to end with the following disclaimer: *The trademarks mentioned in this article are the property of their respective owners.* In other words, the people who own them are the people who own them — even the words that should be generic terms but for some inane reason, Bill Gates has determined that we should capitalize them when we are speaking of his domain.

Airline Travelers' Religion

People pick the funniest things to base a religion on. I bet you never realized that there is an entire religion based on the baggage-checking habits of airplane travelers.

It's true. There are two main sects in this religion: people who *never* check their baggage, and people who *always* check their baggage. Both adherents feel that they have attained some higher state of consciousness because they have discovered the universal truth to the definitive method of air travel. And both can rightly argue that their method is superior and that members of the other "denomination" are obviously doomed to eternal damnation for believing otherwise.

I have always fancied myself as an equal-opportunity apologist. The cynics in the audience will say that's a fancy way of saying that I can argue out of both sides of my mouth. I like to say that I'm "objective" — so much so that I can effectively argue both sides of an issue without giving away my true feelings.

I shall now demonstrate such talent. See if you can determine my true religious leanings based on the contradictory arguments I give:

I always check my baggage

There is no group on the face of the earth that is any dumber than a bunch of passengers loading themselves onto an airplane. There's something about hearing your row called while you're holding a boarding pass that reduces the cumulative IQ of the population by at least 50 points. I want to have no part in the madness.

People lose perspective when they attempt to gauge whether an item will fit into an overhead bin. I've seen people carry on golf bags, horse saddles, and mounted moose heads, thinking they were going to stow them above their heads. Hey, buddy, it ain't gonna fit.

Even baggage that is specifically designed for overhead stowage seems to confound them. What part of "put the wheels-end in first" do they not understand? Folks, you can fit one roll-on baggage in a bin if you put it in sideways. Stow it correctly and you can put three or four in each compartment. Is that too difficult for your feeble minds?

No, I am not going to be guilty of such transgressions. My baggage goes to the nice man with his hand out and palm up at the curb. He takes my suitcase, puts a nice bar-coded ribbon on it, and loads it gently onto a waiting conveyor belt. Miraculously, it reappears on a suitcase merry-go-round only a few feet away from my rental car at my destination. No lugging through the airport and no cramming anything over my head getting dirty looks from all.

My laptop fits comfortably under the seat ahead of me. I fasten my seatbelt low and securely around my waist. And I watch the madness, wondering all the time, "How in the name of the Wright Brothers does that idiot believe that he's going to stow that lampshade in the overhead bin?!"

I never check my baggage

People who check their baggage are stupid, wimps, and incredibly naïve. I can't believe that anybody would actually trust their precious possessions to a bunch of nameless, faceless people on the other side of that conveyor belt who are making minimum wage and are only working in baggage handling because they couldn't be trusted to work with metal detectors.

Did you know that the airline industry loses about 127 billion pieces of luggage a year? And they destroy the handles and straps of at least that many every day. They have a policy about "normal wear and tear" that must have been written by a team of lawyers, guaranteed that they are absolved of all blame.

Besides, when I get off the plane, I want to go where I want to go. What's this idea of having to wait for you baggage to appear, *if* it appears. I'm ready to leave; why isn't my baggage?

No, my luggage stays with me. They always warn people to keep their possessions in their sight and under their control. Well, mine stays with me. It goes where I go when I go there. Under the seat, above my head, in my lap. I don't care. It ain't getting out of my sight.

Conclusion

There, I did it. I successfully argued both sides of a very controversial topic. And I did it in such a way that nobody who reads it could possible tell which side of the issue I'm on.

Nope, none of you guessed that I believe that people who never check their baggage obviously have the IQ of warthog. Here's hoping that their contents will shift during flight, because my contents are safely stowed in the lower levels of the aircraft. I'll calmly pick them up on the way to my rental car, thank you.

Slim Pickins Ain't All That Bad

When I was young, I realized that I had two pairs of aunts and uncles that were related to each other both my blood and by marriage. Aunt #1 was married to Uncle #1 and Aunt #2 was married to Uncle #2. But Aunt #1 was the sister of Uncle #2. And Uncle #1 was the brother of Aunt #2. Nothing incestuous; it's just that a brother and a sister married a sister and a brother.

I thought that was rather odd, so I ask my mother about it. (She was the sister to Aunt #1 and Uncle #2.) She said there was nothing strange about it at all. A one time, it was very common for brothers and sisters to marry among the same families. In the small country church that my mom grew up in, there were only two large families, the "Smiths" and the "Joneses". Since each clan had several children, it wasn't unusual for several of the Smith boys to pick out Jones girls to marry. Heck, there weren't any other families to choose from.

They called it "slim pickins". And the lack of slim pickins is one of the things driving up the divorce rate today.

When the pickins are slim, people tend to be content with what they have. And when things aren't exactly the way they think they should be, they work together to make it right.

When a Jones boy looked across the one-room school house at the Smith girl, he knew that was pretty much as good as it was going to get. And ya know, she didn't look half bad. He could picture little

Miss Smith snuggled up to him at the bonfire after the hay ride on Saturday night. And she looked pretty good.

Soon Mr. Jones and Miss Smith were married. That's when Mr. Jones realized that maybe he had painted a rather optimistic picture of the new Mrs. Jones. But it didn't matter if she put on a few more pounds or left the cap off the toothpaste. She had a big plate of fried chicken ready for him when he came in from the fields. And she kept him warm at night while she soothed his aching muscles. And that kept him pretty happy.

Besides, pickins were slim. What else was he to do?

Today, the pickins aren't so slim. A few strokes of the keys or clicks of a mouse and Myspace, eHarmony, or www.i-wanna-hot-date-tonight.com is all one needs to find an alternative. The choices are abundant; the temptations are inviting; the consequences are few.

Maybe if we went back to our slim pickins and realized what a good deal could be found right in our own back yard, we'd be less tempted to stray and more content with what we have.

Why I Collect Postcards

Guys collect things. There's just something about seeing a bunch of disorganized stuff out there that demands that some order be enforced. It's human nature. It's what makes us different. It's what makes the "chaos theory" apply to geology, but not to the human soul.

Several years ago, I collected baseball cards. What a perfect hobby! There were hundreds of thousands of baseball cards out there and they were practically begging me to take them all in, place them in their proper place in an album, and give them a well-deserved home.

One thing in particular intrigued me about baseball card collecting: the hobby was somewhat finite. You could pick up the newest edition of Beckett and, within some reason, you knew exactly where you stood in your collection. You knew exactly what you had, you knew exactly what you needed, you knew exactly what it was worth.

Baseball card collecting was finite. Been there. Done that.

A couple of years ago, I discovered postcards. It was completely by accident. I was poking around on eBay and I stumbled on a postcard of the church I grew up in. A little more stumbling followed, and I was soon introduced to the hobby in a very serious way.

I discovered an interesting paradox. Postcards are at the same time finite and infinite. On the one hand, there is certainly some number which represents the total number of collectable postcards out there. On the other hand, nobody could ever claim that their collection of postcards — no matter how extensive — is “complete”.

Postcard collecting is one of the most satisfying hobbies I have ever found. Sometimes you find what you believe to be a real “gem”. And it is a gem simply because you say it is. Other times, you find a card that you believe to be “routine”, but a friend of yours will claim it to be the greatest find since the Dead Sea Scrolls! I have had both experiences, and they are equally enjoyable.

Every time you hold a postcard in your hand, you are holding a very, very private part of somebody’s life. Whatever was important to that person when they mailed that postcard is forever inscribed on that thin piece of fragile cardboard. Cherish it; it deserves honor and respect.

Just about every postcard contains two messages — the generic message of the picture on the card, and the very personal message of the person who sent it. That’s why I believe both the front and the back of the card are important. In them both exists not only the slice of life in the picture — but the slice of the person’s life who sent the card.

(Interestingly, postcard enthusiasts — deltiologists — say the “front” of the card is the side with the picture and the “back” of the card is the side with the address. Philatelists — stamp collectors — consider it the other way around; the “front” is the side with the stamp. But I digress...)

Most postcards can be picked up for a buck or two. I've never paid more than ten or fifteen dollars for one. But I'd never sell one of mine for a thousand dollars.

Collecting postcards as a hobby is not only inexpensive, it's flexible. If you just buy a bunch of postcards, you don't really have a collection; you just have a bunch of postcards. But most people don't do that. They collect "themes". I chose my hometown as my theme. But other people buy pictures of old buildings. Or bridges. Or trees. Or street scenes. Or churches. Or hospitals. The possibilities are infinite.

I encourage you to consider joining me in my pursuit of the perfect postcard collection. To learn about the hobby, go to your favorite Internet search engine, type in "postcard collecting" and start reading. Go to eBay and look for your favorite subject. You're sure to find a postcard that can be uniquely yours.

You'll soon discover, as I did, that collecting postcards is truly an infinite hobby.

Superman Can't Read Your Mind

Some of the greatest love lyrics are in the song *Can You Read My Mind?* It was from the original Superman movie with Christopher Reeve and Margot Kidder. This song is amazing because it can be studied on so many levels.

==============================

Can You Read My Mind?
by Leslie Bricusse and John Williams

Can you read my mind?
Do you know what it is you do to me?

I don't know who you are,
Just a friend from another star.
Here I am, like a kid out of school,
Holding hands with a god. I'm a fool.

Will you look at me, quivering,
Like a little girl shivering.
You can see right through me.

Can you read my mind?
Can you picture the things I'm thinking of?
Wond'ring why you are
All the wonderful things you are.

You can fly! You belong to the sky.
You and I could belong to each other.

If you need a friend,
I'm the one to fly to.

If you need to be loved,
Here I am.
Read my mind.
==============================

Superman and Lois Lane are falling in love with each other, but they can't let the other one know about it. Superman doesn't want Lois to love him as Superman; that would be too dangerous. He wants her to love him as Clark Kent. Of course, Lois thinks that Clark is a bumbling fool. On the other hand, as a liberated woman who never had to rely on anybody else for help, she's not sure that she wants to give her heart to anyone, let alone an alien with super powers that she doesn't yet understand.

This is very early in Superman's career. He's not really even a super hero yet. Many people don't understand him. Some people believe he may even be evil. And, although people know he's strong and that he can fly, people don't know what other powers he has. Some have even postulated that he can read minds.

Lois is trying to figure him out. She knows that he can fly. And she knows he has x-ray vision. ("You can see right through me.") But she doesn't know if he can read minds.

So, as a test, she sings this song to herself. (Actually, during the movie, the John Williams score plays softly in the background while Margo Kidder softly recites the words.) "Can you read my mind? Can you picture the things I'm thinking of? You can fly! You belong to the sky! But you and I belong to each other. If you need a friend, I'm the one to fly to. Here I am... Read my mind."

In her mind, she's begging him to understand her. She smiles at him. He smiles back.

The irony, of course, is that he can't read her mind. He has no idea what she's dreaming of.

Why do we feel like we have to play games in relationships? Why can't we just say what we feel? Why can't Lois just declare her love for Superman? On the other hand, why is Superman so clueless that he has no idea what she's thinking?

Such is a microcosm of so many relationships.

The Government We Deserve

The Irish playwright George Bernard Shaw once mused "Democracy is a system ensuring that the people are governed no better than they deserve." He was right. The irony of democracy is that we don't always elect the best person for the job. But we'll usually elect the most appropriate.

One reason is because the best person for the job usually isn't running for election. "Politicians" do a good job of getting elected because, by definition, that's what they do for a living. But they are rarely the best citizens available. And they are not always the best law-makers. They are usually simply the last ones standing — the least of an abundance of evils.

The good news is that — over the long run — things have a way of working out. After a period of time, a consensus develops. It may not be the one that everybody agrees with, but one that everybody can live with.

And that's the beauty of the democratic system. Properly done, no one person or ideology can exceed the generally accepted boundaries of common sense because enough other voices will eventually join in unison to act as a buffering agent. In the end, wisdom will prevail.

In the short run, however, the news isn't always good. The wrong people are often elected. Bad laws are enacted. Corruption erupts. And consequences are suffered.

The next time you are lamenting over the loss of your candidate, or the stupidity of recent legislation, remember the words of Henry Longfellow during the darkest hours of the American Civil War:

"The wrong shall fail, the right prevail."

Things have a way of working themselves out.

Why We Vote

During the American Revolutionary war, a common battle cry was "No taxation without representation." That was a relatively new concept at the time. The idea that the common man should have any right to self-governance was not yet universally accepted. It was generally accepted that the crown was the defender of the land and the insurer of common welfare. To even think that a regular citizen could have a say in matters such as taxation was literally an act of treason.

Over the years, wars have been fought and lives have been lost defending the right to self-governance. We now believe that the power to govern comes from the people, not the other way around.

The right to vote is the ultimate expression of that belief. And it is the duty of all good citizens to inform themselves of the issues and exercise that right.

Don't be discouraged by recent reports of election scandals. Electronic voting and cyber-fast news delivery has only made evident what election officials have known for years. When millions of votes are cast, thousands of mistakes are made. New technology doesn't prevent those mistakes - it only makes them more evident.

When elections results are close, there is a slight danger that such errors can actually affect the ultimate outcome. But those cases are very, very rare. Indeed, it is in those very close that fewer mistakes are made because election officials are even more diligent. And it is in those elections that your vote counts the most.

Don't believe the lie that your vote doesn't count. Learn the issues; know the candidates; do your homework. And then vote. The very future of democracy is counting on you to do your part.

Liberals and Zero-Sum Gain

A caller to a local radio talk show yesterday gave an interesting insight into the mind of a liberal. The call illustrated a common theme that runs through most liberals' thought processes. Liberals believe in the almighty power of the zero-sum gain.

The caller complained that President Bush was not really serious about capturing Osama Bin-Laden. He claimed that the war in Iraq was taking too many resources away from the search for Bin-Laden. If only Bush had not been distracted by the situation in Iraq, he would have devoted all the resources of the U.S. armed forces to the search for Public Enemy Number 1. Obviously, Bush was much more interested in conquering Iraq than he was in fighting the true source of terror in the world.

In the caller's mind, the success of one project obviously contributed to the failure of the other. Or put another way, the failure of one project is obviously the result of the dedication of resources to the wrong place.

In fact, the capture of one individual in a hostile, foreign environment is very much an art, not a science. Of course, when the person does not want to be found and is surrounded by resources that help him evade capture, that makes the job that much harder.

America is full of hundreds of criminals that have evaded capture. On our home turf, there are men that are walking the streets that are currently on the FBI's most-wanted list. If we can't find all of own home-grown criminals, is it such a sin that we've lost one man half-way around the world? Besides, he has been rendered virtually powerless by our anti-terrorist activities. Having him in custody (or dead) would be nice. But having him as a whimpering, sniveling coward ain't half bad.

Liberals have an uncanny desire to celebrate defeat. Their notion is that no victory could possibly be good because it was certainly caused by bad news somewhere else.

They especially don't like the war in Iraq, so it seems to get blamed for everything bad that happens. Bin-Laden hasn't been captured because we're fighting in Iraq. The government couldn't respond to Hurricane Katrina because we're fighting in Iraq. All the cops that President Clinton put on the streets are gone because we're fighting in Iraq. AIDS is running rampant without a cure because we're fighting in Iraq. Every hangnail on every Democratic congressman is the direct result of the war in Iraq.

In fact, the liberals' obsession with zero-sum gain is evident in most of their pet philosophies. Since they do not believe in the creation of wealth, they believe that every tax-break-for-the-rich (to them, it's a hyphenated word) can only be achieved on the backs of the poor.

If I get medical treatment and pay for it myself, that denies some poor soul his due right of medical treatment. If the natural flow of the economy increases gasoline prices at the pump, it means that some oil executive is getting rich. If a college-educated white guy works hard and gets a promotion, that same job has been denied to a poor uneducated black single mother. If a car is built overseas, a Detroit union autoworker has lost his job.

And the list goes on. To a liberal, a butterfly flapping its wings in China is just the beginning of the polar ice caps melting

Whenever you hear a liberal complain about some evil injustice in society, just remember that they are incapable of understanding anything except the most simple of cause-and-effect relationships. The complexities and dynamics of a free society and a growing economy are too much for them to comprehend. It helps when you view their feeble attempts to rationalize life with that kind of perspective.

Ups and Downs of Fashion

Things go up. Things go down. And it's inevitable that things will meet in the middle.

One day, I was picking up my son at school. I was sitting in the parking lot with the car running and the air conditioner on, undoubtedly irritating Al Gore by not remaining carbon-neutral for the day.

As I was waiting, a young high school couple walked by. They were both about 17 years old. She was a tiny waif; no more than 85 pounds soaking wet and probably hadn't eaten anything larger than a cheese cube in the last ten days. He was a good looking clean-cut football-jock type. They would have been a great couple for prom king and queen.

But the odd part wasn't about what they looked like. It was about what they were wearing. She was wearing tan capri pants and he was wearing dapper khaki shorts.

Some of you have already figured out the punch line, haven't you?

His shorts were longer than her pants!

Ya know, it used to be that pants were long and tops were long and shorts were short. That's how they got their names, after all. When I was growing up, our bell-bottom pants literally dragged on the ground. That was a status symbol; the quality of the pants could be measured by how well they were frayed on the bottom. A side-benefit: nobody could tell that you weren't wearing any socks. Heck, nobody could tell that you weren't wearing *shoes*.

Girls' shorts were short and guys' shorts were short. Life was simple. If your knees were showing, you were wearing shorts. Of course that also meant your thighs were showing, too. And the bottom of your pockets hung from underneath the frayed ends of your cutoffs. It was cool. It was the way it was supposed to be.

Once I was flipping channels and I stumbled on that sports classics network where they show games from other decades. An NBA game from the 1970s was on. Those guys had long legs. And short, short shorts. No piercings. No tattoos. No green hair. Just a tank top and short, short shorts.

Oh, and high-top athletic shoes. But those are so retro, they're actually in style again, aren't they? Maybe soon I'll see a 17-year old waif in capri pants, a tank top that doesn't meet her belt, and high-top Keds. Probably with a pierced eyebrow.

Just Another Day on Mercury

Even though Mercury is one of our closest celestial neighbors, we know less about it than most other planets. It has inspired legends and mysteries through the ages and is only recently beginning to yield its secrets. Let's look at this strange little world.

The ancients actually thought there were two "Mercuries". They saw one that magically appeared in the sky just before sunset and another that magically arose in front of the sun just before sunrise. It didn't occur to them that they were actually seeing the same planet on both sides of the sun at different times in the year.

Of course, a "planet" to them was nothing more than a point of light in the sky. That's why Mercury was named for the wing-footed Roman messenger god. Most of the other planets simply "wandered" among the stars. By comparison, Mercury "scooted" — appearing here, then there, then not at all, then back again. Surely, Mercury must have seemed to be the swiftest and most perplexing of all the gods.

As planets go, Mercury is kinda an odd duck. A planet's orbit is never exactly circular, but Mercury's is more oblong than most of the inner planets. In its path around the sun, it gets as close as 25.6 million miles and as far away as 43.4 million miles. In the course of a Mercurian "year" — which is really only about 90 earth-days — the sun seems to slowly "pulsate" in the sky.

Such a close yet eccentric orbit causes another weird aberration: Mercury's unusual day. For years, astronomers assumed that Mercury was "tidally locked" into the sun, i.e., the year and the day were the same length with the same side always facing the sun, much as the moon is tidally locked to the Earth. But we now know that Mercury's day and year are in a strange 2:3 resonance. There are exactly three Mercury days for every two Mercury years.

That means that there are some areas on Mercury that would see the sun rise, then set, then rise again before traversing across the sky. This weird orbital and rotational ballet challenges our very thoughts of what is a "night" and a "day".

Mercury is the only major planet without an atmosphere. Just like our moon, it is rocky and barren, pocketed with craters formed by millions of years of meteor hits and occasional collisions with small asteroids. With no protective atmosphere to shield it, it is literally lying naked to space.

Mercury sits up proud in space. Most planets tilt from their orbit somewhat — such a tilt is what gives the Earth our four seasons. But not Mercury. Its axial tilt is less than 0.01 degrees.

That means that Mercury hosts some of the hottest and the coldest surface temperatures in the solar system. At noon on the equator, the sun is directly overhead and stays in one place for so long that the surface is baked to 800 degrees F — hot enough to melt lead. But at the bottom of some craters near the poles of Mercury, there are surfaces that have never seen the light of the sun for millions of years. Temperatures there hover around minus 300 degrees F and never get any warmer.

For all the mysteries of this planet, only one spacecraft has ever seen it up close. Mariner 10 visited it in the mid-1970s. We haven't been back since. Getting to Mercury is no easy task. Even though it's one of the closest planets, it actually takes more rocket fuel to get there than it takes to go to Mars. That's because once you get there, you have to contend with the gravity of the sun to slow the spacecraft into an acceptable path for scientific purposes. Otherwise, the craft would pass by Mercury in the blink of an eye.

The Messenger spacecraft is currently on its way to Mercury to unlock more of its secrets. It solves the whole orbital gravity problem by looping around the sun a few times, passing the Earth and Venus in a round-about path to Mercury to get it into the right orientation. After a couple of quick fly-bys to Mercury in 2008 and 2009, Messenger will settle into an orbit around Mercury in 2011.

When it gets there, who knows what strange stuff we'll learn about this quirky planet?

My Kingdom for a C-Prompt

For the last few days, I have been reading about "Vista", Microsoft's new operating system that is due to be released the beginning of 2007 (or whenever). I'm especially intrigued by the minimum — that's *minimum* — system requirements just to get this thing installed on a computer. Five hundred and twelve megabytes of random access memory. That's four times the memory that is on the 8-year old computer that I usually use at home.

Ah, my home computer. 128 meg of RAM. 10 gig of hard drive space. A ZIP drive for backup. And Windows 98. State of the art when I purchased it. It's as old as my refrigerator. Almost as old as my pickup truck. Only half the age of my house.

But in computer years, it's ancient. As old as the hills on Grandma's chest. Older than dirt. It's so old, its serial number is negative. The last time I called Dell's customer service, the guy on the phone just sorta chuckled when I told him my model number. I just hung up. He was no help.

So here I am will a moderately functional computer and an operating system that's six versions behind. No upgrade path. No residual value. Scrap value of maybe a couple of bucks if you melt the silver out of the motherboard. But hey, it's paid for.

While reading about Vista, I became more than painfully aware of the limitations of my computer. Last month, Microsoft officially stopped supporting my operating system. According to onestat.com, almost 87% of all personal computers run on

Windows XP. 2.7% run on my operating system. I have never been in such an ignominious minority. For a middle-aged white guy, that hurts.

A long time ago, I was a C-prompt guy. The computer waited patiently for me to tell it what to do. And then it did it. One thing at a time. I didn't have to point at anything or drag anything. It didn't connect to the Internet behind my back and download viruses. It just did what I told it to do.

Sometimes I long for those days. Sometimes I just want a computer to ask me what I want it to do. Then I can type in a command and it will do it for me. Sigh. It'll probably never happen again in my lifetime.

I'm saving up for a new computer. By the time I can afford one of those new-fangled giga-ram computers, Vista will be three of four versions behind. It'll take twenty gig of RAM to load the operating system, which will probably be code-named "Leroy" or something like that.

If I had a kingdom, I would give it up for a computer that had a C-prompt and an operating system that could run on a meg of extended memory with a 32-meg hard drive. Then I'd type on a black screen with green letters in a fixed font.

And life would be good.

The Myth of the Problem with Outsourcing

If I had been in the labor force fifty years ago, I couldn't do the job that I do now — mainly because my job didn't exist fifty years ago. Heck, it didn't exist ten years ago. I work in a very high-tech industry. Most of the people that I work with have jobs that didn't exist even five years ago.

And it's true the other way around, too. Fifty years ago, my mother was a telephone operator. That was back in the days when every small town had a lady named Sarah that would ask "Number, please?" when you picked up the phone. No need to dial; no need to remember esoteric codes or numbers. You just had to say, "Hey, Sarah, could you ring my wife at the office for me?" Sarah would know who you were, who your wife was, and what office she worked at.

My mom's name isn't Sarah, but you get the point.

Nobody cried when modern telephone technology replaced Sarah and my mother. And I won't cry five years from now when my current job becomes obsolete. Because, just like my mom did, I'll find another — a better — job.

And that's the way economic progress works. Why is it that so many union bosses are just now getting it?

When a job is shipped overseas, it's almost always for a good reason. Company owners don't move a job overseas just because they think it sounds exotic. They do it because — for whatever reason —

the lower price overcomes the slower delivery time, the increased transportation costs, and the increased logistics. That's right. The price is so much lower that it's actually worth the extra trouble.

You can make an argument that manufacturing workers over there are that much underpaid. Or that manufacturing workers over here are that much *over*paid. It really doesn't matter. The differential in the labor cost justified the change.

Who benefits? Here's the little secret that not one union member wants you to hear. *Everybody!* Yep, everybody benefits every time a job is moved offshore.

The manufacturing company benefits because the cost is lower. And that almost always means that the price to the consumer will be lower — slowing inflation and giving consumers more money in their pockets and more places to spend that money. Even if the manufacturing division of the company loses workers, the logistics division benefits because managers will be needed to track the production and deliver of the product in this country. The shipping industry benefits because they get to ship the product. And, of course, the foreign company benefits because they get the increased business.

Even the displaced worker benefits because he now gets an opportunity to get out of his buggy-whip manufacturing job and into one that is more suited for today's service-oriented economy. The education system benefits because they get to train the new worker.

And the economy in general benefits because that worker will probably no longer be a member of a labor union — and lower union membership is good for the entire country.

I've been preaching these basic concepts of economics for years. It's finally sinking in. A new study done by two Princeton economic professors was recently presented to a meeting of the Federal Reserve. The paper claims that outsourcing generally boosts wages in America — exactly they opposite of what the traditional labor-dominated liberal egg-heads would want you to believe.

Maybe somebody finally realized that the outsourcing movement has been going on for more than a decade and what do we have to show for it? Inflation under control and virtually full employment — even with an influx of millions of illegal workers in the country.

This is in an economy where your Dodge truck may be made Mexico and your Toyota Camry may be made in Kentucky. The global economy took over while the unions were rearranging the deck chairs on the Titanic.

Please Pity the Poor Penny

The news is finally official. It had been suspected and rumored for a long time. Now the federal government has finally admitted.

It costs more than a penny to make a penny.

This is not good. In fact, it's illegal. Congress has told the US Mint in no uncertain terms that it cannot spend more than the face value of a coin to produce it. It makes sense. If there was more than a penny of value in a penny, people could just buy them and melt them down and sell them for scrap. The Hungarians did something similar to that after World War II when they papered their walls with worthless Hungarian paper money.

But it's not hyperinflation that is the source of the penny's problems. It's the price of copper. There is now almost two cents of copper inside each penny, which is ironic because since 1982, a penny is mostly made of zinc; only about 2.4% of a penny is copper. Nevertheless, it still would cost more to melt a penny than it's worth. But that may not always be true. The mint is going to have to think of a better plan.

Of course, many people think they have solved the problem. Just get rid of the stupid thing. Nobody has been able to actually buy anything with a penny for years. The only thing it's good for is to make sales tax come out even. And nobody would complain if merchants would simply round everything to the nearest nickel. Or dime, for Heaven's sake.

Because of that, many people have taken to throwing their spare pennies into dresser drawers, glass jars, and water fountains. Heck, the Jerry Lewis collection tray at the drive-through at McDonald's is full of them. People seem to be in denial. They just don't want to have anything to do with them.

And that creates a problem for the mint. At the same time that they cost too much to make, they have to make more of them because people are hoarding them. It's hard being a government entity.

I take the exact opposite approach. At any given moment in time, there are between zero and four pennies in my pocket. And none at home. None. None on my dresser. No glass jar collecting spares. No Pringle's can that weighs a ton from collecting worthless copper — I mean 97.6% zinc and 2.4% copper.

Nope. I use pennies the way they're supposed to be used. When I make a purchase that ends in 97 cents, I pull two pennies out of my pocket and hand them to the clerk. If I don't have two pennies, I get three back in change. No more than four pennies are ever — I mean *ever* — required for any cash transaction.

See? Pennies aren't a problem. You don't need a jar of them. You only need at most four.

Oh, yeah, the mint says that a nickel costs more than a nickel to produce, too. They have nothing to fear. I'm not hoarding those, either.

Mike Brown, the Planet Hunter

The surname "Brown" is one of the most common in America. And "Michael" is one of the most common names for men. So it's no surprise that there are a lot of "Michael Browns" out there.

Most of them live in somewhat obscurity. But simple statistics would indicate that a few of them would achieve fame. Wikipedia lists 25 different men named Michael Brown. The list includes politicians, athletes, musicians, and artists.

Two of them are scientists. And one is an astronomer. And Michael E. Brown the astronomer is the subject of today's article.

Mike Brown discovered what may turn out to be our tenth planet. Or our twelfth, depending on how you count them. And perhaps many more.

Mr. Brown is a voracious planet hunter. He's an associate professor of planetary astronomy at the California Institute of Technology and he spends a lot of his time peering at the heavens through Caltech's telescopes in search of planets. In the last five years, he and his associates have been responsible for discovering no few than 10 new bodies of rock and ice hurling around our sun and eligible to be considered planets.

Three years ago, he discovered Sedna. Careful measurements later determined that Sedna was almost as large as Pluto. That news set the astronomical world on its ear.

Once astronomers started looking in earnest for new planets, our time-honored definition of planets started crumbling. It fell completely apart last year with the announcement of the discovery (by Brown and his team) of a new heavenly body, tentatively named. Xena. When the orbit and size of Xena was carefully plotted, yep, Xena is actually larger than Pluto.

Brown's wife proved that a prophet is without honor in his own city. When he called to tell her the news that Xena was larger than Pluto, she said, "That's nice, dear. Can you stop by the store and pick up a loaf of bread on your way home tonight?"

Mr. Brown estimates that there could be as many as fifty bodies out there that are big enough and round "round" enough to be considered a planet. (Potato-shaped rocks need not apply for planet status.) Science textbooks are soon to be re-written on a scale that hasn't been seen in a generation.

Rather than a tightly defined list of exactly nine planets, it now seems that the rocks and balls of gas that orbit our sun exist in somewhat of a continuous spectrum of sizes, shapes, and characteristics. Perhaps there is no limit to the variety of stuff that is out there. Things seem to be a lot more complicated than we first suspected.

For his efforts, Michael Brown was honored by Time Magazine, having been included on its list of "100 Influential People of 2006". Good for him. I'm not a big fan of the magazine, but if they would ever like to recognize my superior blogging skills by including me on a similar list, I wouldn't turn them down.

Shoeboxes of Data

After my formal computer education, one of my very first real job interviews was with a company that produced computer output on microfiche.

For the uninitiated, microfiche is kinda like microfilm, except that the media is a 4x6 card instead of a roll of film. It's a medium that has all but disappeared in common business practices today. It has been regulated primarily to government archives and libraries. But in the early 1980s, it was definitely bleeding-edge technology.

Until then, the process of creating microfiche was strictly photographic and analog. The document was printed on regular paper and then the pages were photographed one page at a time to create the fiche. It wasn't much better than actually standing at a photocopier and recreating the entire report by hand.

But this company was using a new-fangled technology called COM or "Computer Output Microfiche". In this process, the fiche was created digitally, directly from the data source — usually a computer tape. It was much faster and cheaper than the analog process and it could create an unlimited number of perfect images.

In my job interview, I was indoctrinated by two guys who were the microfiche disciples of the company. They extolled the virtues of microfiche over conventional means of storage and lookup. They made a convincing argument that disk storage was particularly expensive and ineffective. After all, it required expensive online disk drives and indexes and the energy and upkeep to keep them running. And horror of horrors, online disk storage required that people have those expensive CRTs at their desk. We can't have that, can we?

Ah, yes, CRTs. Cathode Ray Tubes. Dumb terminals. Essentially, a TV screen with an oversized typewriter keyboard attached. That's what people had before there were PCs on every office desk in the universe.

The compelling argument in favor of microfiche was that you didn't need a $7,000 television set on every desk when you could have one $500 microfiche reader that would serve the entire office. Need to look up a customer's account? No problem. Just walk over to the microfiche cabinet, find the appropriate card, insert it into the reader, search for the customer's page, copy the information to a notepad, and walk back to your desk with the customer still on hold.

That was 1980. It took about five microfiche cards to hold about a meg of data.

I have a memory card on my keychain that holds about a gig of data. That's a thousand meg or 5,000 microfiche cards — enough to fill ten shoeboxes.

For less than a thousand bucks, I can walk to my office supply store and pick up a one-terabyte external hard drive that will plug into the USB port on my laptop. I can tuck the entire drive into a corner of my briefcase. A terabyte is a thousand gig. A thousand keychain memory cards would fill about ten shoeboxes.

Conventional wisdom used to say that bigger was better. All we needed was more shoe boxes. And bigger shoeboxes. In the ultimate irony of technology, we have come to realize that bigger is smaller. And instead of a shoebox, all your really need is a shirt pocket.

A Particularly Perplexing Pill

A few years ago, a friend of mine in the health care industry told me that a man my age needed to take an aspirin every day. Something about thinning blood and preventing heart attacks or something like that.

I have to say that it was a friend of mine that told me to take the aspirin because I never go to a doctor. Never. I can't remember the last time I was at a doctor. I went to a Marcus Welby-type for a few years. Then he retired, as all good Marcus Welby-types do. I haven't had a decent reason to visit a doctor since then.

You know all those commercials where they say things like "be sure to consult your doctor" for whatever? Well, I don't have anybody to talk to.

Back to my story. So I was told by a friend to take an aspirin each day. So I did. No big deal. Later, I found out, oops, not just any aspirin. Think of your sensitive stomach! You want ulcers? It has to be *children's* aspirin.

Really? I had been taking regular aspirin for several months and I didn't notice any difference. No heart attack. No stroke. No ulcers. Just a half-empty aspirin bottle to show for my efforts. (That's why I don't like preventative medicine. How do you know when it works?)

Nope, that's not good enough, said my friend-the-surrogate-doctor. It had to be a children's aspirin. Or at least, it had to be one of those new mini-dose aspirins.

Mini-dose aspirins? Yeah, it seems that so many middle-aged men were being advised by their doctors (I guess they actually had doctors) to take children's aspirin that there was a rush on the stuff. But a lot of guys didn't like the idea of taking "children's" aspirin.

So the marketing suits at the drug companies came up with a brilliant idea. Let's make children's aspirin but put it in a bottle that says "Mini Dose". Same drug. Different label.

It was a hit. Soon millions of men in America were relieved of the embarrassment of buying the kid stuff. Now they could get real he-man drugs. Little bitty, tiny pills.

Okay, so I went to the store in search of the new drug. Hmmm... I guess this is it. But look at the size of the dose. 81 milligrams. Eighty-*one*? What's the deal with that? Why not an even 80? Or 100? What's the business about a silly milligram more?

Back to me friend with the question *du jour*. That's just the way it is, I was told. A mini dose is 81 milligrams. Get used to it.

Never one to be satisfied with an answer like that, I had to do some digging. This is what I found out.

A standard aspirin is 325 milligrams. Back in the days before children's aspirin, parents were instructed to split an adult aspirin. And then split it again. The kid was to receive one-fourth of the original pill.

When children's aspirins came around, it seemed logical to introduce a pill that was exactly one-fourth the size of the adult aspirin. Well, technically, 325 divided by 4 is 81.25. I guess they figured the extra quarter milligram was taken up in the dust left behind on the kitchen cabinet when the pill was split. Whatever. The drug companies weren't going to quibble a quarter milligram, but by golly, they were going to get that extra milligram in there.

So a children's aspirin is 81 milligrams only because the drug companies are good at math and they like rounding.

When the adult mini doses appeared, it made sense to manufacture them in the same molds that were used for the children's aspirins. So the 81 milligram adult mini aspirin was born.

Doesn't matter. I take them every day. I still haven't had a stroke or a heart attack. Or an ulcer. Or an upset stomach, headache, diarrhea, night sweats, fainting spells, or anything else. I still operate heavy machinery any time I feel like it.

And I still don't have a doctor to call my own.

Vote to Win: A Bad Idea

The state of Arizona will consider on its November 7 ballot an idea which should be soundly defeated. It's an idea that is so patently absurd that I'm surprised that I even have to write an article condemning it. But registered voters signed referendum petitions in sufficient numbers over the summer to get this stupid idea on the ballot. So the whole state is going to vote on it in the next general election.

The idea: Pay people to vote.

Actually, the plan is that each person who votes in either the state primary or general election will be given a chance to win a state-run lottery. The grand prize of the lottery (actually, the only prize) will be a cool one million dollars.

Proponents of the plan claim that their goal is to increase voter turnout by giving people something tangible as a reward for their vote. Apparently, these people don't realize that participation in the democratic process is supposed to be a reward in itself.

Neither side of the debate has forgotten that federal law prohibits making or offering of any "expenditure to any person, either to vote or withhold his vote." Fans of the law claim that the chance to win a million dollars has no value because it is just that — a "chance", not actually any compensation.

Well, they're wrong.

Any statistician, economist, accountant, or casino operator will tell you that the probability that an event will occur contains an inherent value. It is the value of the event multiplied by the likelihood that the event will occur.

I'll use very round numbers for demonstrative purposes; the concept is the same. If four million people vote and receive a chance to win a million dollars, each chance is worth exactly twenty-five cents. To say that it doesn't have a value mocks the intelligence of the voting public and denies basic fundamentals of mathematics.

That's right, they would serve the same purpose if they just handed everybody a brand new Arizona-commemorative quarter at the polling place. And they'd probably make more people happy at the same time.

Even if this hare-brained idea could pass legal muster — which it can't — I would still question the wisdom of attempting to use such methods to increase voter participation. That makes the assumption that increased voter participation is always a good idea.

In fact, if incentives such as this are enacted, all it will guarantee is that more people will vote that wouldn't have voted otherwise. People will vote who haven't studied the issues. They will vote without any idea of who the candidates are. Many will vote without even being able to read English. Many will turn in blank ballots or ballots that will have to be invalidated because they voted for more than one candidate for the same office. Some people will just make random marks on squares on the ballot. They'll do it because they have no interest in exercising their right to vote; they just want that million dollars.

In fact, I can envision the worst possible scenario. A couple of days before the election, the Democratic Party will release advertising with the following message. "Confused about who to vote for, but still want to be entered in the lottery? No problem. Just vote a straight Democratic ticket! That lets you vote for all the best candidates with only one stoke of the pen."

The biggest problem is that the proposal incites the very people to vote who actually have the least valid reason for voting. The least educated, the least informed, and the those least interested in the democratic process are the ones that would be most drawn to this type of incentive. I don't want to deny them of their right to vote; but I see no reason to offer them special incentives to do so.

Let's hope that wisdom prevails among the voters of Arizona and this measure is defeated. It's a bad idea.

Related to the Pope

A recent Associated Press article illustrated the intertwining of the generations, using actress Brooke Shields as an example. It seems that the lovely Ms. Shields is related to Charlemagne, William the Conqueror, Niccolo Machiavelli, Hernando Cortes and at least five popes.

The point of the article is not that she is distinguished by her pedigree, rather that such a pedigree is completely normal. Anybody that lived more than a few hundred years ago probably had a half dozen or more children. As such, they undoubtedly have millions of ancestors today.

It is estimated that at least 80% of the population of England is directly descended from King Edward III, who reigned 700 years ago. Even six U.S. presidents can be counted among his descendants.

The Mongolian conqueror Genghis Khan spread his influence — as well as his seed — almost as far as the Holy Roman Empire. Traces of his DNA have shown up literally on all corners of the world.

So we don't have to go all the way back to Adam and Eve to prove that we're all "cousins". But that's not what struck me about the Brooke Shields article. I got hung up on the fact that she was descended from five *popes*.

When I first read that, my feeble Protestant mind started protesting. Waitaminnit. Aren't popes actually people that received the ultimate promotion from priesthood? And isn't a fundamental tenant of priesthood one of *celibacy?* And if one is celibate doesn't that make it kinda hard for him to have, uhm, *descendants?* This certainly required further investigation.

I discovered that the Catholic Church considers celibacy to be a *discipline*, not a *doctrine*. It wasn't until around the year 800 that they decided that a celibate lifestyle was the only acceptable one for a priest. Prior to that, several popes had been family men in quite the literal sense. Even after that, there were a few popes that married and fathered children before they entered the priesthood. In those cases, they can rightfully claim descendents.

And there were a few popes that were just scoundrels. Popes that had illegitimate children (or at least illicit affairs) during their papacy include Pius II, Innocent VIII, Alexander VI, Julius II, Clement VII, Benedict IX, and Pius IV.

It has been claimed that Clement II died while being treated for a venereal disease. And Paul III was said to have postponed his own ordination so he could continue his promiscuous lifestyle, spawning the Protestant Reformation in the process.

In fact, nepotism was so rampant with the pre-reformation popes that several of them were father-son combinations, handing down Peter's keys to Heaven much like a father might hand down a dry-cleaning business to his son. Maybe it's not ironic that the word "pope" is taken from the Latin "papa", which means "father".

So, Brooke, rejoice in your heritage. There's a good chance that your family tree — as well as mine — includes a cacophonic mixture of royalty, papacy, mass murderers, world explorers, and shepherd boys. Mixing all that DNA over the course of a few generations contributes to the fact that we are all unique in our own little way.

The Pool Ain't Cool

We're coming up to the hottest part of the year. And once again I hear the same insane comments from people. No, I'm not talking about the stupid *it's-not-the-heat-it's-the-humidity* comments. Those are bad enough. I'm talking about people that think the best way to beat the heat is to go swimming.

"It's so hot today. All I want to do is get in the pool."

Excuse me. The *last* thing I want to do when it's hot is to be in the sun. *Outside.*

I know where these people got their idea. It's from the Depression. Back then, everybody was poor and nobody had air conditioning. The movie theatres put blocks of ice in front of electric fans to cool the audience. Yeah, I bet that was a treat. But that's all they had.

Combine that with the drought, dust-bowl conditions, and record-breaking heat of the early 1930s and you can see that people were looking for whatever they could to stay cool.

So they slept on their porches. They slept on their roofs. They slept in the city parks.

And during the day, they cast off their inhibitions and went to the pool. After all, it was the coolest are in town.

Not any more. The most comfortable place in town right now is my living room. 72 degrees. Or whatever I want it to be. It doesn't get any better than that.

When I drive by a swimming pool on the hottest day of the year, I see a lot of people having a lot of fun. Nothing wrong with that. They're laughing and playing and splashing and generally having a good time. Good for them.

They're also sweating, but they probably don't know it because their too wet from being in the pool.

One thing they're *not* doing, however, is keeping cool. They're hot, they're just having too much fun to realize it. They're playing in the sun, for crying out loud. Nobody is keeping cool by staying in the pool. They're just keeping their mind off how hot it is.

So if you want to go to the pool on the hottest day of the year to have fun, go for it. God bless you; if that's the kind of exercise you believe is fun, who am I to stop you? Just don't tell me that you're going there to "cool off".

Next January, when it's ten degrees below zero, I think I'll suggest that we all go to an outdoor community campfire so we can stay warm. That makes as much sense as going swimming to stay cool.

The Art of Telecommunications

Have you noticed that radio transmission towers have lately become more ... well, more *interesting*?

Before I go further, I had better define a couple of terms. Those tall skinny things supported by guy wires with their regulation FAA blinking red lights are not radio antennas. Technically, they are towers. The antenna is just the thing that sits on a tower. Sometimes an antenna sits on the very top; sometimes they are hung on the side. Antennas come in all shapes and sizes. They may be long and slender, they may be spherical or oblong, they may be boxy, or they may be flat.

It's the antenna's job to actually transmit and receive radio signals — usually from another antenna far away. The only purpose of the tower is to hoist the antenna into the air to make it more effective.

And lately, it's the antennas that are making the towers interesting.

Long ago, transmission towers were primarily the domain of commercial radio and television stations. They were impressive; tall and skinny. Well, that was about it. The taller they were, the skinnier they appeared to be. Straight up. About as aesthetic as a pencil lead.

A few years ago, more and more of them started sprouting on the landscape. And these newcomers were different. They had *character*.

Suddenly, the tops of the towers sprouted wings. Instead of one boring antenna on top, just about every imaginable antenna could be found. Many times, several different types were on the same tower. They jutted from the sides, they sprang from the top, they ringed the midsection.

The thing that made the difference, of course, was the sudden ubiquity of mobile telephones. Now that there are millions of wireless devices roaming around out there, thousands of new transmission towers are required to communicate with them.

Wireless phones have different transmission needs than a regular commercial radio. For one thing, the communication is two-way, unlike your car radio. It's also full-duplex — which means, unlike a CB radio, the phone can send and receive at the same time.

And other "housekeeping" transmissions have to occur, which you may never be aware of. These are telemetry signals that help the network keep track of where the phones are and whether or not they are turned on and available to receive a call. They also tell a phone when to ring.

And mobile telephones are only part of the wireless communication revolution. All types of wireless devices demand similar communications networks. Blackberries, GPS devices, satellite radio signal repeaters; even the computer that I'm typing this article on is plugged into a virtual wireless network and is in constant communication with a tower down the street from my house.

Of course, such complex communications require complex antennas. And in the process of building them, the communications companies inadvertently gave us new works of art. To make it even better, many of them have banded together to put multiple communications systems on one tower. The same structure may contain antennas belonging to Sprint, Verizon, Cingular, and a couple of other local carriers. Each antenna adds its own special flavor to the total picture that makes every transmission tower unique in its own way. And that makes it unique art — high in the rural sky.

The next time you're zooming down the interstate, look up. There are some really neat high-tech patterns of wires, steel, and fiberglass up there, ready for your viewing pleasure. After you have enjoyed it, don't forget to thank your wireless provider for the show.

How Cars Move — And Why they Don't

Have you ever been stuck in traffic and wondered why nobody is moving? I'm not talking about heavy traffic where you crawl down the interstate at 20 miles an hour. I mean where as far as you can see *nobody* is moving.

Barring some sort of obstruction in the road — like a major accident or a giant meteor — how can that be possible? If everybody is pointing the same direction on the same road and wanting to get to the same place, how can everybody be sitting still?

This was the question on millions of minds last fall as they attempted to "race" out of New Orleans while Hurricane Katrina was barreling down upon them. Highway officials had reversed the traffic flow on the interstates so extra lanes were available to leave town. Everybody had plenty of warning and they were all essentially going the same direction, i.e., *away* from the city. So why did they spend so many hours just sitting on the highway?

The same thing happened a few weeks later as Hurricane Rita took aim on Houston. Tempers flared, cars overheated and ran out of gas, but for the most part people found themselves just sitting on the highway for hours at a time.

There's a simple answer for this. Although cars are generally built to move very fast, they do not maneuver very quickly when they are in close proximity to each other. The closer together that cars are, the more awkward they are and the slower they are driven. It doesn't matter that they are all going the same direction. It really doesn't even matter if there are a lot of merging lanes. A congested highway is a slow one.

It's easiest to understand this concept if we put it in human terms. Let's say we're at a major league football game in a packed stadium filled with 75,000 fans. In the middle of the game, an announcement is made that everybody must leave. But half the exits are blocked, so everybody needs to leave via the exits on only one end of the field.

Oh, and there are a few restrictions around leaving. The most important restriction is that nobody can touch anybody else. No touching. At all. Period. You can't brush against each other, you can't touch elbows, you can't even place your hand on somebody's shoulder.

To make sure nobody touches each other, you should keep a reasonable distance from each other — at least three to eight feet. No closer than that. And when the person next to you moves, you should wait two to five seconds before you begin to move.

That's what it would be like if we applied the rules of the road on a human scale. Under normal circumstances, a large stadium could be evacuated in half an hour or so. My guess is that if we all had to act like cars, it would take all day to get everybody out of there. And there'd be a lot of people just standing around for a long time.

Another Parent Trap

Every male who as ever seen Disney's 1961 version of "The Parent Trap" has fallen in love with Hayley Mills. There's no way you could get around it. Who wouldn't fall for the girl with a big grin bouncing back and forth with her hands innocently behind her back as she sings "Let's Get Together, Yeah, Yeah, Yeah"?

Even girls would have to admit that Brian Keith would make a really cool dad in his country ranch house in northern California. I honestly believe that this is one of the most perfect live-action movies Disney ever created — with the possible exception of "Mary Poppins".

So why in the name of Walt did the Disney studio believe that this gem needed to be re-made in 1998? Oh, I know. Let's make money with a proven product. Yeah. Well, I'll have no part of it. When the new version came out, I had absolutely no interest in it. Nothing was going to mess with my perfect image of Hayley's Susan and Sharon.

Nothing, that is, until it showed up on cable TV and my son wanted me to watch it with him. No, no, no, don't watch *that* version! Let's rent the *real* one. You know ... *Hayley!*

Nope he wanted to watch this one. So I relented.

Actually, it wasn't too bad. This one was a launching pad for Lindsay Lohan in the dual role of Hallie and Annie. This was a pre-teen Lindsay, when her hair was really red and her freckles actually frecked. She definitely showed promise as an actress.

She even hummed a few bars of "Let's Get Together" in homage to Hayley.

The most remarkable piece of acting was that she pulled off a proper British accent for Annie. In the original movie, Hayley's British accent was never really explained. Heck, it just added to her charm. In the new version, Annie was raised in London by her mother while Hallie was raised in California by her father. Lindsay did a wonderful job of switching accents seamlessly.

And, of course, technical standards have improved greatly in the last 45 years. Whereas Susan and Sharon's shots seemed rather contrived and stilted, Annie and Hallie interacted with each other in front of a panning, zooming, and tracking camera with perfect ease. It's amazing what they can do with electrons in Hollywood these days.

But dangit. Some things just shouldn't be messed with. Just ask the guys who remade "The Poseidon Adventure". The ship only overturned but the movie sank quicker than the Titanic. And remember that shot-for-shot re-do of "Psycho"? Sicko.

So Lindsay pulled it off and went on her way to a very successful career in the process — re-working "Freaky Friday" and "The Love Bug" along the way.

But I really wish the suits in Hollywood would realize that some things — such as fond memories in an old man's heart — are really just better left alone.

Hopefully, This Will Satisfy the Purists

Being somewhat of a linguistic snob, I take notice when I am accused of puncturing the Queen's English. So I was somewhat taken aback when I was privately chided for my use of the word "hopefully" in a recent article. I have chosen to come to my own defense.

In the purist sense, "hopefully" means "in a hopeful manner". It is not to be used casually as a replacement for "I hope" or even the more passive and stuffy "it is hoped that".

For example, it may be okay to say. "She gazed down the street hopefully, wondering if her lover would ever return." But it's not proper to say, "Hopefully, the math teacher will be sick and we won't have to take that algebra test tomorrow."

Well, that may be true. But I think that ignores the fact that occasionally we need small pauses in casual writing to allow the reader to grasp the true meaning of what's being said. Actually, I just demonstrated it. And I just did it again.

Most people read faster than they should. When that happens, the words tend to overflow their comprehension buffer. Words mindlessly enter their consciousness without being adequately considered, studied, pondered, and comprehended.

When writing in a casual style, sometimes the author needs to plant little devices into the text to slow things down. Kinda like linguistic speed bumps. They aren't exactly "noise" words because they actually provide some extra meaning to the sentence.

But they require a little extra mental processing, which in turn slows the mind down. If these little gems weren't sprinkled through the text, the reader would be, in effect, "over-driving his headlights", venturing into uncharted territory without proper guidance.

For some reason, adverbs fit that bill very well. An occasional "actually", "really", and yes, even "hopefully" can be used in that fashion. Not only do they provide a little emphasis or clarification to the subject, but they provide a brief pause in the action — a time for the reader to reflect on what has just been said and to anticipate what is to come.

Of course, any device like that can be overused — especially in casual conversation. I once worked with a guy who began every sentence with "basically". It didn't provide any meaning or clarification. It didn't enhance or give any credibility to what he was about to say. It was just a bad habit. A dreadful habit, actually.

In one meeting, several of us threatened to throw a stapler at him the next time he began a sentence with the word "basically". He looked at us — quite terrified — and never said another word the entire meeting.

Actually, it was a very pleasant silence. Hopefully, he learned his lesson. Really, he had it coming.

Straight Shootin' Dick

Vice President Dick Cheney is a guy of not many words. He's also a guy that isn't running for any election. You can tell that because he doesn't need to soften his words when confronted with a liberal interviewer. No spin for Dick; just the facts, ma'am.

Consider this little clip from a recent interview with CNN's Wolf Blitzer.

Blitzer: Do you think Hillary Clinton would make a good president?

Cheney: No, I don't.

Blitzer: Why?

Cheney: Because she's a Democrat. I don't agree with her philosophically and from a policy standpoint.

Blitzer: Do you think she will be president?

Cheney: I don't.

Blitzer: Who do you think will be?

Cheney: I'm not going to speculate.

Blitzer: Will it be John McCain?

Cheney: I'm not going to speculate.

That's what I like. Straight to the point...

Would she make a good president? *Nope.*

Why? *She's a Democrat.*

Think she'll be president? *Nope.*

Shades of Herbert Hoover.

Cheney gets criticized for being too corporate. Well, yeah, he was the CEO of a Fortune 500 company and was on the board of several other companies.

Anybody with a resume that looks like that doesn't need to be political. No punches pulled, no bushes beat-around here. He shoots straight. (Just don't go duck hunting with him.)

When Cheney was tapped for the veep job, he didn't need it. He didn't need the money. He wasn't seeking fame or lime-light or glory. He had no legacy that he had to write.

He decided to serve his country. Pretty admirable, if you ask me. And since he expects nothing in return, he feels no need to play politics with the media.

Reporters beware. If you ask Dick Cheney a question, expect an answer. Quick. Direct. Truthful.

In contrast to Bill O'Reilly, the spin doesn't stop here. Nothing was ever spun in the first place.

Liberals Say the War Isn't Over

I was prepared today to write an article congratulating liberals on their victory. I was going to say that they had won the civil rights war; there was no longer any reason to continue fighting it.

As evidence that they had won, I was going to point to the federally-mandated observance of Martin Luther King, Jr.'s birthday. Dr. King is the only human being that we honor is this method. We do not honor any president on their birthday. (We used to; we had separate holidays for presidents Washington and Lincoln — just watch Bing Crosby in "Holiday Inn" to see how they used to do it in the 1940s. But it was too inconvenient to have two holidays so close together, so they were morphed into a single celebration, supposedly honoring all presidents.)

We don't honor any other birthdays. Not even the birthdays of liberal bastions like Franklin Roosevelt or John Kennedy or George McGovern. No liberal is worth of such tribute. None except, of course, Dr. King.

And in typical liberal fashion, we don't actually celebrate anything he *did*, we just celebrate the fact that he was *born*. We don't celebrate each August 28, the date he delivered his famous "I Have a Dream" speech. We don't celebrate each March 25, when he led the famous march to Montgomery. Surely these — or any number of similar events in his life — would have been worthy of note.

No, liberals are never interested in what people actually *do*. One's intentions, their wealth (or lack of it), or their heritage is sufficient for notice.

Of course, that's in direct contrast with King's dream that his "four little children will one day live in a nation where they will not be judged by the color of their skin but by the content of their character." True liberals are not interested in judging people by the content of their character. Their love of affirmative action policies proves that they would much rather judge people by the color of their skin.

As I was saying, I was prepared to congratulate liberals for winning. They had successfully used the birth — not the accomplishments — of a great American and perverted his message in a way that merely stretches the already-too-long Christmas holiday by another two weeks while doing nothing to advance the causes for which Dr. King so fervently fought.

I was going to congratulate liberals for winning, until I read about their surprising admission that they were, in fact, losing. That admission came from the deep south that Dr. King loved so much. It came from Shirley Franklin, the African-American Democratic mayor of the great city of Atlanta.

Ms. Franklin took to the pulpit of Ebenezer Baptist Church, the very church where Dr. King was once pastor. Instead of celebrating the victories of the last half century that Dr. King had worked so hard for, according to an AP article, she admonished congregants not to pay tribute to King's dream on his birthday and then contradict it the next.

Millions can't find jobs, have no health insurance and struggle to make ends meet, working minimum wage jobs... Thousands of black and Latino students drop out of high school believing education will not matter. And statistics say it doesn't because they can't find jobs.

Yep, it isn't good enough to have a black associate on the Supreme Court and a black Secretary of State. It doesn't matter that the richest woman in the history of television entertainment is black. It doesn't matter that no black has been denied attendance to a college or the right to vote or told to sit in the back of a bus in fifty years. It doesn't matter that almost half of all professional baseball players are black, sixty years after Jackie Robinson broke one of history's most famous color barriers.

No, liberals such as Ms. Franklin point out as evidence that the war has not been won the fact that black high school dropouts who understand rap music better than the concepts of balancing a checkbook have a hard time finding a job in a growing economy with virtually full employment.

Mayor Franklin, you are correct. As long as you keep reminding blacks of their failures and their shortcomings, the war will never be won. With people like you in power, Dr. King's legacy is indeed one of defeat.

Mr. Baldwin's Winter

It's been one of the warmest winters on record in New York. For the first time since 1877, no snow was recorded in New York City for the entire month of December.

Actor Alec Baldwin used the occasion to advance his personal liberal agenda. Writing in the Huffington Post blog, he said "All around us are signs of global climate change. And this Administration's response is to send in more troops. If you don't think there is a link between the weather and Iraq, you are wrong."

Two weeks later, New York state was digging out of a record 100-inch snowfall.

Wow, I didn't know George Bush was empowered to increase the world temperature by two degrees in a century, which somehow raised the temperature in New York to thirty degrees above the average, which in turn crystallized all the water in Lake Huron and dumped it on the Adirondacks.

Liberals and other global warming Chicken Littles fail to understand one basic concept of global climate science: the Earth's temperature is not nearly as stable as they'd like it to be. And it never has been.

But their hatred of George Bush and anything capitalistic and entrepreneuristic blinds their better judgment into believing that a war on the other side of the world causes hurricanes on this side. (They literally salivated at the prospect of another Katrina last year and were publicly disappointed when the Atlantic went an entire season without depositing one significant tropical depression on our shores.)

The 10th through 14th centuries were warmer than “average”, which gave rise to the term “Medieval Warm Period”. That was followed in the 16th to 19th centuries by a period of cooler than “average” temperatures, now known as the “Little Ice Age”. What comes next? Yep, warmer temperatures. Duh.

This is in spite of the scare that we all endured in the 1970s of the threat of “Global Cooling”. Remember the Nuclear Winter that we were all going to face because of the carbon emissions of the time? Now those same carbon emissions are being blamed for a warming trend.

Guys, the main source of the heat of the Earth is the sun. The sun gets warmer, the temperature goes up. The sun gets cooler, the temperature goes down. It’s a big, big sun. Really, big. That means that it has a rhythm, but it’s a very, *very* slow rhythm. It takes it a long time to get a few degrees warmer and then a few degrees cooler.

Accurate temperature records measured with mercury thermometers were virtually non-existent before 1880. If a weather station moves across town (as it has in recent years in Los Angeles and Kansas City) the “average” temperature can fluctuate by ten degrees or more. You can plant a tree near a thermometer and lower its temperature reading. Or you can build a sidewalk near it and raise it. But none of those events have global impact.

You can count all the tree rings you want to, but nobody could have measured the temperature five hundred years ago with the accuracy of today.

And what of Mr. Baldwin's snowless New York? Well, it's the warmest winter in New York since 1877. Oh gee, Alec, I guess that means it was warmer 130 years ago than it is today. Are you going to blame that winter on George Bush, too?

The Richification of America's Poor

It is a well-established fact that the poorest of America's poor is wealthy when compared to the poor of most other countries. But that fact is lost on liberals who depend on the poor for their political survival. The constant redefinition of "poor" is the very foundation from where they derive their power.

In the thirty-one years between 1973 and 2004, the U.S. Census Bureau tells us that the percentage of people in America living in poverty "grew" from 11.1% to 12.7%. Did that mean that the billions of dollars spent on raising people from the depths of poverty has been wasted? Nope. It just means that the liberal egghead bureaucrats have done a great job of raising the poverty level each year to make sure a sufficient number of citizens fail to clear the limbo bar of prosperity.

Senator Ted Kennedy likes to refer to those "poor" as people who "go to bed hungry each night". He and his fellow liberal legislators fail to understand the basic principle of algebra that says that if you define the bottom ten percent of your population as "poor", then about ten percent of your population will always be, uhm, poor. Duh.

Let's look at some facts about America's poor that the think tank Hoover Institute uncovered.

Half of all households under the poverty level has cable television and at least two television sets. A fourth of them own a personal computer. Most of them own a VCR or DVD player.

Friends of mine who teach school tell me of students on free lunch programs wearing hundred-dollar designer tennis shoes and sporting fully-loaded iPods and GameBoys.

Half a century of Great Society reforms has bred a generation of sponges that take pride in beating the system while living in a luxury that the richest citizens of most third-world countries could only dream of.

How do we stop such abuses while still providing an adequate safety net for those who are truly needy? I think the answer lies in the numeration of the luxuries of those receiving aid. I propose a simple plan. With a little tweaking, it just might work.

In my plan, certain "luxuries" would be denied to those receiving federal aid. Simply put, if you are receiving food stamps or Medicaid or welfare payments, there are some things that you simply cannot buy.

For example, nobody receiving federal could subscribe to cable TV. Period. Cable providers would be required to submit a list of their subscribers to federal agencies who would match them against lists of recipients of certain federal programs. A letter would be sent to all households that match. They'd be given a simple choice: TV or federal money. You can't have both.

Same for cellular phones. You want a phone? Give up your monthly check.

It wouldn't have to stop there. Why should they be able to rent movies? No Blockbuster or Netflix memberships for these people. If they want to watch a movie, they can relinquish their government subsidy.

Magazines? Nope. There is no need for the poor to read TV Guide, Reader's Digest, Playboy, National Inquirer. None of them. In my system they could have their choice: magazines or a check from the government. But not both.

Things like magazine subscriptions and cable service and Blockbuster membership — those would be easy to enforce. But heck, I honestly believe that the technology exists to prevent individual purchases, too.

Purchases of any shoes over fifty dollars would be off-limits to welfare recipients, if I had my way. The same goes for ice cream, grocery store bakeries, fine deli meats, and sugar-ladened breakfast cereal. And certainly no alcohol or tobacco products.

Entire stores would be off their list. They wouldn't be able to buy anything from Starbucks, Crate & Barrel, or any department store fancier than JC Penney's.

I think it'd be a good idea to force at least 80% of their purchases to come from Wal-Mart. Well, maybe Wal-Mart and Target.

Please understand that I believe in a capitalistic society where everybody should be buy what they want to and shop where it suits them. It's not my intent to actually deny anybody any freedom. But when you accept federal money, you need to check your capitalism at the door.

I think everybody should have a right to buy all the fine things in life. I just don't want them to do it with my money.

Hillary Wants to Take It — All of It

Do you own anything? *Anything?* You might as well hand it over to Hillary Clinton. Right now.

She is currently the odds-on favorite to become the 44th President of the United States in 2008. And she has just declared that she wants it. All of it.

What is "it"? While speaking at the Democratic National Committee winter meeting, Hillary made this chilling statement:

> "The other day the oil companies reported the highest profits in the history of the world. I want to take those profits and I want to put them into a strategic energy fund that will begin to fund alternative smart energy alternatives and technologies ..."

Those are six stunning words. Words that should never be uttered in public. Certainly never by an elected official...

"I want to take those profits."

They send chills up my spine.

Just whose "profits" does she think she's "taking"?

Mrs. Clinton, with all due respect (actually, with a total disregard for respect, but that's just a polite thing to say), corporations don't earn profits! They can't. By their very definition, the profits belong to the *owners of the corporations.* In a capitalistic society, we refer to those owners as *stockholders.*

If you have money in a bank, if you have money in a mutual fund, if you have money in a 401k or an IRA, if you have attempted to put away a little bit of money for your retirement years — there is a good chance that you are a stockholder. *And Hillary wants to take your profits.*

Hillary doesn't want to take the profits from some nameless, faceless, fat-cat puffing on expensive Cuban cigars. She wants to take money away from you. She just doesn't have the guts to admit it.

She has already identified several industries that — in her mind — don't deserve to exist. Their role is better done by Big Government. They include the oil industry, the health care industry, and the pharmaceutical industry. At least. Big government has already taken over the education industry. Can transportation be far behind? Communication? Farming? Construction? Manufacturing? Where does it end?

"I want to take those profits."

Well, Mrs. Clinton, there are a few profits of yours I'd like to take.

As a United States Senator, you earn a salary of $165,200 every year. I want to take those profits.

In 1979, you turned a $1,000 investment in cattle futures into a $100,000 profit. I want to take those profits.

In 1996, you wrote a best-seller named "It Takes a Village", which earned you hundreds of thousands of dollars. I want to take those profits.

In 2000, you earned an $8 million dollar advance for your book *Living History*. I want to take those profits.

Watch out, people. Hillary is coming after you. She wants to take your profits. She thinks they belong to her.

FactCheck Has Company

You can measure the credibility of an organization by noting how much it's interested in achieving its stated goal, rather than in taking credit for it.

For example, if an organization is dedicated to curing cancer, would it not rejoice if cancer was cured by a competing organization? Or would it try to discredit the cure, or inhibit the progress of finding the cure?

Moving from cancer to politics — not much of a stretch, actually — our collective hats go off to FactCheck.org, the arm of the Annenberg Foundation dedicated to keeping politicians honest, and to informing the public when they are less than so.

FactCheck.org rose to fame in the 2004 Vice Presidential Debate when Dick Cheney accidentally referred to them as FactCheck.com. Although a certain George Soros web site suddenly got a lot of hits, the confusion was cleared up the next day and I suddenly became a fan of this wonderful site.

It is the purpose of FactCheck.org (emphasis on the ORG!) to check on all the things that politicians say in public — both mundane and outlandish. When the outlandish is discovered, FactCheck.org (emphasis on the ORG!) rushes into action, publicly chastising the politician and setting the record straight. They are entirely non-partisan; Democrats and Republicans get equal treatment. They have no bones to pick; nothing to sell except the truth. It is truly American politics at its finest.

So I was pleasantly surprised when an email landed in my inbox from FactCheck.org (emphasis on — oh, I'm tired of that joke already) with the subject line, "We Have Company!"

That's right FactCheck (dot whatever) is actually announcing the arrival of their competition. And, in true character with the organization, they couldn't be happier.

The St. Petersburg Times has started a new web site, PolitiFact.com. (Yep, they're a for-profit newspaper; dot-com is okay.)

Whereas FactCheck.org deals mostly in the hard truth (or fiction) of an item, PolitiFact.com attempts a little bit of qualitative judgment by assigning each item a "Truth-o-meter" rating. This unique 6-level scale rates each fact from "True" through "Half-True" all the way to "Pants on Fire!"

PolitiFact.org has been known to get slightly whimsical at times. Joe Biden's comment that "The president is brain-dead" got an unmerciful "Pants on Fire!" rating, noting that brain death is defined as "irreversible unconsciousness with complete loss of brain function". Gee, lighten up; I think a little poetic license in political rhetoric is acceptable.

But the point is that FactCheck.org welcomed the competition with open arms. Gotta give them credit for that. In a time where everybody is clambering for their share of the pie, FactCheck.org says the water's fine, come on it.

FactCheck.org has always gotten my vote for their unbiased reporting and diligent quest for the truth. Once again, they have shown their true colors. They are more interested in getting the facts out there than they are in taking credit for it. And I admire them for that.

The Postlude

There you have it. That wasn't so bad, was it?

As I said, if you disagree with me, you have the right to be wrong.

But at least now you know what's on my mind.

— Joe